KWAJALIEN
TO
KARACHI

BRUCE LINDER

outskirtspress

DENVER, COLORADO

Kwajalien to Karachi

Outskirts Press, Inc.
http://www.outskirtspress.com

ISBN: 978-1-4787-4651-5

Outskirts Press and the "OP" logo are trademarks belonging to Outskirts Press, Inc.

*To my wife, Georgia,
who wanted the story told*

Contents

INTRODUCTION

STROLLING ALONG A quiet shopping street in downtown Karachi, Pakistan on a warm, sunny afternoon, suddenly several young men come running full speed down the middle of the street. Soon, many more come barreling by, then a huge mob. This doesn't look good. I try to duck into a shop. Too late! The shopkeeper has already pulled down the metal security grating over the front door. There is no one visible inside the store. I try to melt into the store entryway. Now police come running down the street after the mob. The civilians that can't run fast enough are mercilessly beaten with lathi's, bamboo sticks with metal tips that the police wield with great dexterity. An open truck of police with their rifles pointed out the sides of the truck stops directly in front of me. There is a rifle pointed at my midsection from about ten feet away. The policeman has a big grin on his face, in essence, telling me that in the noise and chaos, he could pull the trigger and no one would even notice; just another body to add to the twenty or so others that didn't survive that day. After what seemed like an eternity, the police truck moves on. The whole business was triggered by a political rally for an opposition candidate for the presidency, which had been held in a nearby sports stadium. It was just another unusual day in Karachi.

Two thirds of the way around the world on a tiny tropical atoll island in the middle of the Pacific Ocean it's a rainy night. Sitting around waiting for the ICBM missile launch from Vandenberg AFB in California, I get a call from the control room of our radar saying that the azimuth tracking signal of the radar is intermittent which means that we can't track the missile. Our radar on Roi-Namur Island, Kwajalien Atoll in the Marshall Islands is the prime receiver on this mission. A hold of the missile launch costs the US government one million dollars an hour due to aircraft in the air, overtime pay, etc.

A scrub of the mission would be unthinkable. To make a long story short, here I am crawling out on a narrow antenna feed horn support 45 feet above the concrete roof of the radar building at night in the rain, tapping on the rigid coaxial azimuth signal line, trying to find the source of the intermittent signal. The offending piece of coaxial line was found and repaired before a hold had to be called in to mission control. I like to think that I earned my pay that night.

These are just two examples of the unusual events that occurred over a period of 40 plus years in a career that included lengthy stays in Brazil, Chile, the Marshall Islands, Pakistan, Saudi Arabia, and numerous other stops along the way. In the process, many lessons were learned, some of which may have value to others.

Much of the information that would be helpful to have a productive and meaningful life you may never know about. Some of the information you will hear, but will discount as untrue or unimportant because there is so much nonsense floating around that you may not recognize its value. In this book there is life-changing information that you may not hear any place else. Hopefully, you will recognize it.

This book chronicles the strange adventures of the author and includes insights that he has been allowed to obtain through a series of unusual situations that included:

1. A work assignment in Karachi, Pakistan, as the only American, teaching microwave radio equipment that I had never seen before during a time of government upheaval and revolution.

2. Being in charge of a multi-million dollar proposal to be written in Portuguese in Sao Paulo to the government of Brazil.

3. Being put in charge of an operational satellite station in Chile at night with very limited knowledge of the system and almost no knowledge of the Spanish language.

4. Taking over a failed, long term, countrywide troposcatter communications testing effort in Saudi Arabia and successfully completing it.

5. Working on a ballistic missile defense radar system with no previous radar experience on a tiny tropical island in the Pacific.

6. Hired as a transistor circuit design engineer, never having actually seen a transistor.

7. Assigned to supervise 45 engineers and manage a test and development effort on a shelterized air defense system having no knowledge of the system.

8. Buying hardware and software for and maintaining a large computer development system with no computer background or experience.

9. Working on a highly classified software and hardware system development and implementation with no related work experience.

10. Finding a method of greatly increasing overall health, including much improved eyesight.

CHAPTER 1

THE EARLY YEARS

GROWING UP IN a small town on the plains of South Dakota, there was one overriding goal. Escape! Bitterly cold winters, hot humid summers, and no economic opportunities were definitely not my thing. My family had lived in a small town in western Washington for three years so I had first hand knowledge of a warmer and more scenic place to live.

Due to an unpleasant and confrontational home life, self-reliance was learned at an early age. There was no one to back you up or take your side. Not in my wildest imagination would I bring a school problem or any other problem home with me. You learned to deal with it.

At age nine my parents finally allowed me to have a newspaper route. It was hard to understand why they resisted, because from then on I paid for all my expenses other than room and board. To make more money I wound up with three newspaper routes. Delivering newspapers in the dead of winter was unpleasant to say the least. Later on I became the janitor for the local Woolworth's store. In the summer I would work at the local college in the agricultural departments.

The Lutheran Church had a powerful influence in my early life. I was required to go to Sunday school and then to a church service by my mother. In the summer vacation time I was required to go to a "Vacation Bible School" class in the morning for two weeks. Later, over a two-year period Saturday mornings would be taken up with a "confirmation class." Our minister wanted every confirmation class member to attend a weeklong summertime religious camp in the northern part of the state. Having previously attended the camp, I was not about to go for an encore. The dormitory was crowded with no amenities, the food was very mediocre, and the cost above my pay scale as a newspaper delivery boy. Attempts at embarrassment in front of the class by the minister failed to get me to sign up. During one of our classes the minister pointed out that on average fifty per cent of our class would leave the church. With this level of early indoctrination the church must be doing something wrong. In retrospect a good sense of right and wrong was obtained from my early religious training.

At the age of twelve with my older brother's help, I bought my first shotgun. In the fall my brother and later on, my classmates and I would go pheasant and duck hunting. It was not only fun, it also helped to relieve the boredom and provide meat for the evening meal.

Having a shotgun came in handy on another occasion. My father, who was one of the meanest bullies that I have ever known, used to enjoy picking on my older sister in particular. One Sunday morning they had a conflict about using the kitchen to make breakfast. Dear old dad swatted my sister with a hot spatula. Coming out of my bedroom to go pheasant hunting, I was carrying my 12-gauge shotgun. There was dad glaring at my sister, who was crying and had a large red welt on her arm. Enough was enough. After calling the rotten bastard a few choice names, I pointed the gun at his chest, pumped a shell in the chamber (a sound unmistakable to shotgun hunters) and made a show of taking the gun off of safety. Dad was made to understand that if he ever bothered my sister again, I would blow his head off. He never bothered her again. Come to think of it, he was also nicer to me. It was a shame that I didn't figure this out sooner.

Living in a small town in South Dakota was not an exciting adventure, but there were ways to pass the time. A group of my friends and I hung out at a local pool hall. The attraction of this one particular establishment was that they would serve beer to anyone over the age of about 15, the legal limit being 18. It seemed to attract guys that liked to shoot pool, drink beer, hunt, and play basketball. No college students patronized the place for some reason. One night a friend and I walked in and there lined up on both sides of the place were about 40 high school-aged kids. It appeared that it was some sort of an out-of-town gang confrontation. There wasn't much in the way of gangs in those days. My friend and I began shooting pool with the two opposing groups absorbed in watching us play. Suddenly, my friend looks up as if he just noticed the two groups and says who are these guys? I played the straight man and said it looks like two rival gangs. He said are they going to fight? I said nah, they look like talkers not fighters. That was the spark that sent them out of the place to a rumble outside of town; my friend and I taking credit for starting a riot.

There was a fellow who would stand up at the pool hall, probably after a few beers, and give political speeches. Usually, no one could figure out what he was talking about. One Saturday afternoon we got the bright idea of making his day. As he was delivering a firey political rant, two of the bigger guys picked him up and carried him out the front door on there shoulders and down main street with about 25 of us trailing behind with raised clenched fists, chanting, "Omar Dobbs for president!"

The local college's home coming week was always filled with a lot of partying. It was culminated by a rather impressive parade, which attracted large crowds, followed by a Saturday afternoon football game. One night during home coming week my friends and I were driving down the main street, which was filled with drunken college students. After creeping along with students banging on the hood of our car, we final got to the bottleneck, where two guys were squared off against each other with their shirts off. It gets cold there in November. I rolled down the car window and yelled hit that SOB! A full-scale riot ensued. It's nice to be needed.

Early in life I realized that the playing field was not always level. It was obvious, that certain students were favored by some of the more entrenched teachers. This did not become important until high school when grades would have an impact on getting college scholarships. In an American History class I got the highest grade on all the tests in a six-week period, but received a B on my report card. When I asked the instructor in class why, he explained that coloring maps was a part of the grade. Obviously, my map coloring was awful. From the knowing looks of some of the other students, it was clear that I wasn't the only one that was dubious of that explanation. It became clear that if your parent was on the school board, a faculty member of the local college, and/or was part of the Lutheran Church power structure, you got some help with your grades. A friend of mine would record test score results of the girl who sat in front of him in chemistry class. He always had a higher score. He got a B; she got an A. Her father was on the school board and was also a college faculty member. I had a knock down, drag out argument in class with the same chemistry instructor over grades. He finally yelled, "You missed an A by 20 points!" My very quiet response was, "but you gave me a C." There was no apology.

There were certain teachers that I simply could not get an A from. The dishonesty extended to the various school elections. If one of the favored students was running for some office, they always won. Just for kicks, I incited all the assorted student troublemakers to vote for a male student, who was obviously gay, for homecoming queen. We had the votes to win, but of course, his name never came up in the balloting.

In my junior year I was one of four boys to be selected to go to Boy's State, a week-long work shop about how government works, etc. It was a surprise to me as I was the only one who was a rabble-rouser; the other three were goody two shoes. Good grades were a requirement, which eliminated a lot of the other students. Just for kicks I ran for some office so I could get up in front of the whole group and give a speech. It was humorous, and I got a few laughs. The whole week was mildly interesting. We were taken to a Class C baseball game one night for a little entertainment. It was bitterly cold, so another attendee and myself cut out and found a cafe nearby and drank beer while we were thawing out, although we were both underage.

Some friends and I went to an out of town high school football game. Just I was coming out of a restaurant carrying two six packs of beer, our football team was entering to have their pre-game dinner. Our side got hammered 33-0. The story was that I had demoralized the team by carrying beer out of the restaurant. You can't make this stuff up. Since I wrote the sports stories for the school newspaper, the team was praised for their valiant effort and only losing 33-0. No one noticed the sarcasm. I was a prolific writer for the school newspaper, even winning an award for the number of lines of copy that I had written. Therefore, it was a little surprising that I was the only senior who was not allowed to work on the high school annual. That was perfectly fine with me, as the poor devils spent many long nights to produce the document. The faculty advisor for the annual was one of those instructors that didn't give out A's to just anyone. It wasn't until years later that I noticed that no mention was made of the intramural basketball team that I had captained being undefeated. Instead, there was some fictitious nonsense about a post-season tournament. Maybe, it had something to do with my providing nicknames for the teams, which were the brand names of prophylactics, in the school newspaper. It took someone four weeks to figure that one out. Maybe no one read the school newspaper.

There was a contest every year about the United Nations. A question list was provided ahead of time. Just for kicks, I entered the contest and was absolutely certain that I knew every answer. A girl, whose father was on the school board, won the contest. Since there was no money involved, I didn't bother questioning the result.

The local college, which would later become South Dakota State University, provided "practice teachers" for six weeks, who were in their senior year and planned to go into teaching. I always tried to be well behaved in their classes, because it was their first effort at teaching. They didn't know or care who the favored students were so they judged the students only on their knowledge of the subject matter. Since I was one of the few students who bothered to read the lesson,

I was always treated well. The same could be said of the substitute teachers.

But it was not always a one-way street. Our chemistry instructor would be in his second floor chemistry lab at night. Who knows what he did there. As I passed by on my way to the local pool hall, I would lob a snowball through his open window. In the winter we would try to find someplace warm to play basketball. Sometimes a door at the high school would be left unlocked. When the chemistry instructor would come roaring down to the gym to kick us out, we would have a lookout posted and by the time he got to the gym, it would be dark with no sound. The solution to the problem was to put a metal bar and padlock on the gym circuit breaker panel. With my slender hand and arm I was able to reach in and turn a circuit breaker on and play would commence. Again, he would come roaring down to a dark and quiet gym. He probably thought that he was losing his mind.

Natural gas lines were being installed in town and kerosene lamps were put out at night to mark the ditches. On Halloween, two of my friends and I gathered up a flock of lamps and put them in the chemistry instructor's front yard, which lit it up as bright as day. I am not sure if he ever connected the dots.

My two older brothers had conflicts with a few of the high school's teaching staff. My first day in class was sometimes marked by dire warnings from the instructor that he would have his eye on me, and I had better fly right. Of course, challenging instructors in their class-rooms about grades did not make me one of their favorites either. We had one instructor who was particularly nasty. My bother Julian had tangled with him a couple of years earlier. The instructor decided to unload on me one day in class for no apparent reason. He also point-ed out that next year I would be taking a course from him required for graduation. It was not hard to incite the class troublemakers to make his life miserable outside of the classroom, as they were not fond of him either. He was gone the next school year. On the first day of class his successor gave a ten-minute harangue on how bad I was, but he was willing to give me a fair chance, etc. But by now I am catching on. My response was, "Have I done something wrong?" We actually felt a little sorry for him. I nicknamed him Snerd after Edgar Bergen's puppet, Mortimer Snerd. My younger sister said that five years later, he was still referred to as Snerd by the students.

One night while roaming around with three other troublemakers, we noticed a huge papier-mâché elephant in front of the downtown auditorium. There had been a Republican political rally that night. We tried to "borrow" a flat bed trailer from a rental lot to haul it up to Snerd's house, but the trailer hitch didn't mate with my friend's car hitch. So the four of us carried the elephant 10 blocks down the middle of the street. We had to put it down about every 70 feet or so because it was so heavy. We expected at any moment to run into the local police, but saw no one. It was a very sleepy town. We placed it right at Snerd's front door. We never heard a word about that caper.

One afternoon a friend and I walked by a grocery store and noticed Snerd was inside shopping. We went inside and excitedly told the store manager that Harold, aka Snerd, the infamous shoplifter, was in his store. The three of us would peek around the end of an aisle to see if we could catch him in the act and then race down to the end of another aisle and continue the surveillance. Maybe it was a slow day for the store manager.

One of our forms of entertainment was to try to pick up college girls, who would be walking back to their dorms from the downtown movie theaters. We would always have some beer to entice them. Our success rate was not real high, but it was fun trying.

A friend and I were hanging around the college one night and stumbled on to a beauty pageant. As we sat watching the event from an open fire escape door, we noticed that the contestants would go through wardrobe changes. Being curious, we found the changing room and raised the window shades slightly. When they would leave the stage, we would race down and view the costume change. They all had really nice figures.

For my senior year in high school I had two classes that would produce a grade of B at best and two where an A was possible. I vowed to never take a book home to study. No matter how cold it was, every night I would go shoot baskets at a hoop in our neighbor's driveway. It was the most enjoyable and relaxing year in school to date. Grades that year were two A's and two B's as hoped for.

One more high school story:

One night, an equally misguided friend and I were doing an activity that was probably against the law. The local gendarmes swooped in, and we narrowly escaped. Standing out in the evening air, we were reliving the adventure and trying to decide if the cops were just trying to give us a scare or were they really that incompetent; we decided on the later. Suddenly, my friend points to the sky and says, "What's that!" Coming towards us are three lights that seem to be reflecting off a metallic surface. They are moving slowly at maybe 1000 feet. The lights seem to be on the leading edge of an object that is blotting out the stars as it goes by, but we could not determine its shape. It seemed much larger than an airplane. There was no sound. It was definitely not a bird, a plane, a weather balloon, or even Superman. My friend went to school the next day and spread the story about seeing a UFO. Knowing about the ridicule that would be coming, when asked, I denied any knowledge of the event. In the US anyone who sees something unexplainable in the sky is said to "believe in UFOs." If you see a helicopter flying by, you don't "believe in" helicopters, you see a helicopter. You may "believe in" the Easter Bunny or the Tooth Fairy. It is strange that if you witness a crime being committed, your word can send someone to prison for the rest of his life. But, if you are one of the millions of people who see and sometimes photograph strange flying objects, it cannot possibly be true. No doubt a lot of people warned Christopher Columbus that if he sailed west, he would fall off the edge of the earth.

South Dakota was the only state in the union that didn't issue driver's licenses. I was working in the summer at the local college in the agricultural department that grew hybrid seed grains for farmers. The boss said to take the one and a half ton truck out to the fields and collect the work crew. No one asked if I had ever driven before.

Fortunately, the straw boss drove the truck back in. Now that my driving credentials were established, one of my assignments was to drive out by myself to a field five miles on the other side of town and irrigate a couple of acres of hybrid corn. I had to climb down a steep bank to the river's edge and start the irrigation pump. After awhile it was time to move the irrigation pipes. The corn was tall and I had to lift the pipes up over my head to reposition them and then start the irrigation pump again. The whole procedure was a little spooky for a fifteen year-old kid, who had never really driven before. Once I stopped by our home and got my younger sister, Carol, to keep me company.

On graduation night from high school a friend of mine wanted to drive to Madison, Wisconsin where his brother was going to graduate school at the University of Wisconsin. We drove all night. The idea was to work there during the summer. Unfortunately, you had to be 18 to work in Wisconsin, but I did land a job working in a Jewish summer camp for boys on Lake Mendota. The food was good, but the pay was so-so. It was a delight, however, as part of the kitchen staff, to beat the junior counselors, who were college students, at softball and basketball.

I soon learned not to mention where I was from. People would take delight in ridiculing South Dakota, although Brookings, my hometown, had the largest university in the state. It usually turned out that those people themselves came from some little jerkwater town.

CHAPTER 2

COLLEGE DAYS

VERY EARLY ON I realized that the ticket out of South Dakota was a college degree. Because of our difficult home life, going to college in my hometown didn't seem like a good idea. I decided on the University of South Dakota (USD). I had been saving money to go to college for years but had lent money to my sister, who was going to college while living at home. Also, the new owners of the local coal company refused to extend credit. It gets cold in South Dakota come November, so I lent money to my mother to buy coal. I am not sure how I had become the family loan company.

On arriving at USD in Vermillion it soon became apparent that there were two kinds of students: Those that belonged to sororities and fraternities, a.k.a. "the affiliates" and the "non-affiliates" or independents. It was easy to spot the affiliates from their superior and condescending attitudes. Some of the independent students referred to the fraternity members as "frat rats." The "frat rats" seemed to major in drinking and chasing sorority girls. They were not much competition for good grades. This did not make for a pleasant atmosphere. This situation did not exist at the college in my hometown, South Dakota State College (SDSC). There was one notable exception to the "us and them" relationship at USD. When the sorority girls got to be seniors and had not found a husband, they became noticeably friendlier.

When I was a freshman at USD, the basketball team won the

small college national tournament.

In the school newspaper there was an article saying that after the victory, "the affiliated students forgot their affiliations and mingled freely with everyone." Hopefully, they even spoke to their fellow "non-affiliated" students. My brother and another student wrote an excellent letter to the editor of the school newspaper warning that this "forgetting of affiliations" could get out of hand. The other student got cold feet so I signed the letter along with my brother, and it was published in the school newspaper. This was sure to be viewed as a not too subtle, nasty dig directed at fraternities and sororities. I remember walking across campus and meeting fraternity members who I had been in class with every semester. It was beneath their dignity to even say hello.

On occasion, I would return to my hometown and hang out with my hunting and drinking pals. They were attending college but most were not very studious. For a reasonable fee of ten dollars I would take their final exam in a class that I had previously taken. I made a few badly needed dollars and their parents were pleased that they passed the course. It was interesting that when playing poker or socializing with the SDSC students, they were friendlier than my fellow students at USD, where I attended school, although the two schools were bitter sports rivals. The problem was probably the "us versus them" fraternity/independent divide at USD.

On one visit home two of my pals and myself decided to go ice fishing in the dead of winter. Towing an ice fishing shack late one afternoon, we managed to get the car stuck in a snowdrift on this lake in the middle of absolutely nowhere. Realizing that we would probably freeze to death by the time we walked to a farmhouse for help, the only solution was to dig the car free. Luckily, the driver had a shovel in the trunk of the car and after a lot of hard work, we managed to free the car and ice shack.

Things were rather boring at USD, especially if you didn't have much spending money. There were Sioux Indians going to school there, paid for by the federal government. The few times I ran into one of them, they seemed like nice people. Two of them offered to do yard work for the local jewelry storeowner. They proceeded to murder the jeweler and his wife, and then continued doing the yard work, a very strange story.

As a freshman I got a job working in the Medical School for the head of the Biochemistry Department running an X-ray diffraction machine for DNA research and was able to work there all four years. He allowed me to coauthor a research paper and present it at a scientific conference. I also had a job in the Physics Department. While working there a graduate student was grading test papers. He mentioned that the head of the department told him to lower the test score of one of the students. This student later said that it was the only B he had ever gotten, otherwise he was a straight A student. I was taking a physics class during summer school and got the highest test scores on all the tests, but received a B. The instructor, who I also played tennis and chess with, said there were no A students in class, so much for grading on the curve. The rather strange head of the Physics Department has some screwball idea of turning USD into the MIT of the West. This somehow tied into the grade reduction efforts. However, during my 40 years of working no one ever wanted to know what kind of grades I got in college.

It was a miracle that my brother, Julian, and I did not starve to death at USD. I worked 20 hours a week and with getting a few scholarships, I was able to survive. USD doubled the tuition fee every year that I was there. We lived in a 8x24 foot trailer that my sister had bought for us, and she also was loaning us money. The government student loan program had just started up my junior year, and I was able to tap into that, which helped a lot.

Unfortunately, not many companies came to USD to recruit graduates. The few that did were usually located in Minnesota, which was every bit as cold as South Dakota. Doing graduate work in physics seemed like a worthy effort and a ticket out of the state. The head of the Physics Department at USD said he thought that he could get me in at the University of North Dakota graduate program. Wow, not as cold as the North Pole, but not my cup tea. It seemed that January first was always very cold. While watching the Rose Bowl football games on TV, the fans could be seen sitting in the stands with their shirts off. The question kept coming back, "What am I doing here?" I settled on the University on New Mexico (UNM) in Albuquerque because they offered me a summer job, a teaching assistantship, and it is warm there.

I spent an enjoyable year at UNM. My only teaching duty was a three-hour physics lab once a week. Some of the physics graduate students were fun people and good tennis players, and we had a great time. I actually had a nice looking girl friend, something that I couldn't obtain or afford at USD.

The Physics Department felt that they had too many students, so to weed them out, they gave out C's in the required seminar class, which is failing in graduate school. Never mind that you were doing well in your regular classes. The hardest physics class was Classical Mechanics and was attended by graduate students at all levels, including students that had been in graduate school for several years. On the first test I noticed that there was a problem that was similar to one that I had run across in an old, obscure physics book, that I found in the library. On the following tests I was always able to get one problem correct by studying the library book, which in this class meant a passing grade. They were very stingy about giving out advanced degrees, keeping students there for years as low cost labor for their research projects. It was time to move on.

CHAPTER 3

DALLAS

I WENT TO work in Dallas as a transistor circuit design engineer for a large electronics firm never having actually seen a transistor. It seemed like it would be fun to learn. Very little of the knowledge, that I obtained in school, would be useful for my upcoming career. At the "welcome aboard" meeting the head of engineering informed the new hires that "You can come in and work anytime you want. We never close our doors." Hmmm, either that meant unlimited paid overtime or else slave-labor. It was all downhill from there.

My first assignment was at the Addison Airport on the outskirts of Dallas, where the company had rented office space in an unused hangar. During lunch one day with three other engineers, one of them said to me, "You don't belong here." It was hardly a ringing endorsement of the company.

My first salary review was terrible. Later, I was to learn that it was because I did not work long hours. For the next six months I came in nights to supervise technicians, layout draftsmen, and wiring girls, all of whom got paid overtime, because the company was concerned that they might unionize. I was certain, that the technicians with their overtime pay, were making more money than I was. For the next salary review I got the same miserly raise of 1.5%. When I pointed out how well we had done, and that the company got a large contract based on the test equipment that we had designed and built, the response was that I had good people working for me. Another engineer on the project that I was on worked insane hours and was routinely praised by management. He reluctantly confided to me that he got a 4% raise. If he had gotten a second job of driving a taxi at night he would have made a lot more money. Of the many insanities experienced during my 15 months at this sweatshop, one of my favorites was that the company provided free coffee and donuts in the morning. A loud bell would ring and you would run like hell to the coffee urn to get your goodies: managers, secretaries, engineers, draftsmen, etc. trying to get near the head of the line. You had exactly ten minutes to get back to your desk, drink your coffee, and eat your donut. When the ten-minute bell rang my supervisor would peer over his cubicle wall to see if anyone was still drinking coffee. It didn't bother the company any that you were expected to work 50 hours a week, if you were caught up. We were never caught up.

Sitting at my desk one day, a nice looking young woman, whom I had never seen before, stopped by and sat down on my desk. There was a shortage of chairs. There were probably no more than five women working in our building out of 300 or so employees. After a couple of conversations, she asked if I minded picking her up in the mornings so she wouldn't have to wait for a bus on the cold winter days. It was only a block out of my way so why not. We dated a few times and I soon realized that the purpose of our friendship was to make her boy friend jealous so he would close the deal. If I proposed first, I probably would have gotten the nod. She was from NYC and had been a flight attendant, but apparently had no luck finding a husband. She was just a little too cold blooded for my taste.

One of the very few pleasures that I had was when I was in my boss's office being quizzed in a hostile manner about a transistor circuit design. After excusing myself to take a phone call, which was a job offer, another engineer walked into his cubicle and resigned. I then had the pleasure of walking in and also resigning.

There was usually at least one good snowfall each winter in Dallas. The morning after one, I was driving on a mostly deserted divided highway. For kicks I was fish tailing back and forth across the two lanes, just having some fun. The oncoming traffic would honk wildly, probably thinking a deranged person was driving. They had never seen such wild driving in the snow.

While carousing around Dallas, I would sometimes drive through the black section of town late at night in an open convertible, not giving it a second thought. There would be crowds standing around. There was never a problem. These days that would probably not be a good idea.

Driving to work one morning on a busy four-lane road in my open convertible, I got broadsided by a woman that ran a stop sign. My car spins across all four lanes of traffic hitting the far curb and ricocheting back across the four lanes, winding up in the wrong direction in the lane that I had been driving in. By some miracle no one hit me. The only thing the woman had to say while waiting for the police to come was that she was going to be late for work! When the arriving cop got about 15 feet from her, she blurted out, "I looked left and I looked right and that's when he hit me." My response was, "Yeah, with the side of my car." Had she been apologetic, we might have chalked it up to experience. But as it was, I wanted to be compensated for the near death experience and grief that she had caused. At work there was a somewhat shady technician, who I asked if he knew any shady lawyers. He did and the lawyer got me an appointment with a doctor, who X-rayed my back from different angles. At a follow up appointment the doctor explained that hardly any one had a perfect spine and that it is not possible to tell when a problem had occurred. I had a vertebra that was slightly tilted. He put his finger on it and said asked if that hurt. It did and he dictates to the nurse that the patient complains of pain in the tilted-vertebra area. The lawyer said the insurance company would settle out of court right before it went to trial for X amount of dollars. He sent me a check for that amount minus his fee, case closed.

One day while getting my haircut I realized that the two barbers were Sioux Indians that had gone to the Flandreau Indian High School near my hometown in South Dakota. They were trying to remember the basketball coach's name. When I mentioned his name, they didn't seem overly surprised that a customer in Dallas would know that.

After escaping the job from hell, I went to work for a small firm near Dallas. We were treated well by management, but still had to work insane hours at times. When complaining to my fellow engineers, I was told, "you are an engineer, and are expected to work long hours." I could see myself in 20 years putting up with this crap and being married with a family, no way Jose.

While playing bridge at lunchtime at work one day, someone walked in and said President Kennedy had just been shot. We thought he was joking, but we had a TV set in the office and turned it on. The newsman was standing there crying so we realized that what he said must be true. When they were transferring Oswald from one jail to the other, my girlfriend and I were standing outside the receiving jail along with a good-sized crowd. While hoping to catch a glimpse of Oswald, we heard a siren. I said to my girlfriend, "someone got him." Emotions were running so high that we assumed that a law officer must have shot Oswald. It was absolutely beyond belief that the police would allow some civilian like Ruby to get near him. There was a question going around Dallas. How did the elephant get into the Jack Ruby trial? The answer was that he snuck by the Dallas Police Department.

Now fate intervenes big time:

A fellow engineer absolutely insisted that I should interview with RCA, who was in town recruiting, for an overseas job at the Kwajalien Missile Test Site in the Marshall Islands. He and another engineer had already interviewed. Partly to humor him, I went to an interview. It soon became apparent that the job was mine, if I wanted it.

Now comes the fun part:

1. There would be an 8% raise. The interviewer apologized for the small amount.
2. There would be a 40% bonus.
3. Room and board is free, but to ease the pain there would

also be $4/day per diem. This was a long time ago.

4. There was overtime pay usually around 10-12 hours/week, which came out to be almost time and one half. Yes, paid overtime!

5. Most of the salary was free of federal taxes.

6. Four weeks of vacation a year plus one week of travel time. Standard vacation time was usually two weeks in those unenlightened times.

7. One free trip to Honolulu plus one trip to your home of reference, which everyone selected as New Jersey, since it was the farthest away, per year. We usually cashed in our airline tickets in Honolulu and went to the Orient or wherever.

8. Free medical and dental care.

My last night in Dallas a bunch of guys from work took me out to dinner, which I thought was very nice of them. I mentioned to the guys that since I was leaving, I would clue them in on my favorite hang out where there were always a lot of women. When we first arrived, they couldn't believe it. After a few minutes, they began to realize it was a lesbian bar. They thought it was a blast and insisted on staying and shooting bumper pool. In walks a young couple with an older couple behind them. The older couple was no doubt the parents of one of them. They were obviously there to show the parents the degenerates in the big city. One of my friends said to the younger male, "If you smile like that again, I am going to kiss you." After horrified looks, the two couples departed, satisfied that they had witnessed truly depraved behavior. My friend was married with small children at home.

After checking in at the RCA Service Company headquarters in Cherry Hill, New Jersey, I was sent over to the RCA Moorestown facility to interview with the radar design expert. He quickly determined that I knew very little about radar operation, which my resume would have told him. He must have figured that I had something on the ball, because after some wrangling, no objections were raised to my getting the job.

CHAPTER 4

BOSTON

I WAS SENT to the MIT Lincoln Labs in Lexington, Mass. to witness the testing of low noise parametric amplifiers, the type of device that I had been designing in my last job in Dallas. Parametric amplifiers are used to receive low-level signals such as radar returns and radio telescope signals. My arrival in Boston was not a good omen of things to come. Arriving in a blinding snowstorm, I missed the turn off from the airport to Storrow Drive, which is very easy to do in the best of times. After driving on a narrow, two-lane road, which was jokingly called a state highway; I eventually got to my motel. The trip had been further complicated by several traffic circles. Unfortunately, you couldn't tell which exit of the traffic circle was the state highway. My rental car was stolen from the motel that night. Hertz did not seem surprised.

In suburban Boston, at that time, there was no such thing as a furnished apartment. In Dallas you could rent a furnished apartment by the month; the choices were endless. I always picked a place that had a lot of women's names on the mailboxes. I was able to find a room in a large house that also served meals in Lexington. Coffee shops did not exist. It turns out the establishment was also a half way house for a mental hospital in nearby Belmont. Most of the renters were mental patients. The patients were usually more fun than the working stiffs. The owner would often ask visitors that ate with us on occasion who they thought the patients were and who were not. They often picked me as a patient. Maybe I had learned to blend in.

There was a four-man team of Western Electric field engineers staying at the half way house that traveled all over doing electronic installation and modification work. They mentioned that while living in the Boston area; they felt that they should be getting a foreign-service bonus. After staying there a while, I agreed with them whole heartily.

The owner of the half way house had a nice summer home on Cape Cod. She would invite the tenants to spend the weekend there. We would go to the local grocery store and select our own lobster and she and her staff would cook supper. I was also carrying on a romantic relationship with her twenty year old daughter, which made life even more enjoyable. On one such weekend getaway she had invited three mental patients from the Belmont hospital who had not been out of the hospital in twenty years or more. I wound up playing bridge with them one evening. Fortunately, nothing unusual happened. Even in normal settings, bridge games can get confrontational. That night I was assigned to sleep in the living room. Needless to say, it was a very light sleep.

When I got to Lincoln Labs, the parametric amplifiers were not working properly because of a vibration problem caused by the action of the liquid nitrogen pump that was used to cool the amplifiers to lower the noise figure. The mechanical engineer who was supposed to be helping was feuding with the design engineer and was no help at all. I was given the task of fixing the problem and testing them with no help from anyone else.

A side note that occurred while at the Labs was that I was allowed to visit a large radio astronomy antenna site run by Lincoln Labs. As my tour guide was pointing out the features of the site, I noticed there was a large work boom that the antenna was on a collision course with as it was being rotated around. I yelled at my tour guide, and he went racing into the control room and had the antenna stopped just before it hit the work boom. God only knows what it would have cost to realign the antenna. I think my guide thanked me, but I am not sure.

CHAPTER 5

KWAJALIEN

AFTER SIX MONTHS everything was working and tested. It was off to the Kwajalien Missile Test Sight, now the Ronald Reagan Missile Test Sight, in the Marshall Islands. I stopped by Dallas on my way. It turns out that I bailed out of the small company near Dallas just in time. When the executives of the parent company paid a surprise visit, they found the company president, who was a Ph. D. and a very scientific type, on the sofa in his office with his secretary. They had forgotten to lock the office door. The company had been losing money, which the parent company understood; but the accountant and the president were cooking the books to make things look better. That was the final straw, and the company was being liquidated.

Flying in to Kwajalien for the first time is a unique experience. Looking down from the plane you see this tiny island and say to yourself, you must be kidding. I am going to live on this little rock?

The Kwajalien Atoll is an interesting place. The lagoon is 20 miles wide by 40 miles long, the largest lagoon in the world. The border of the lagoon is a coral reef dotted with small islands, which are covered in palm trees and lush vegetation. The location was no doubt selected so that the re-entry vehicles from the ICBMs that were shot from Vandenberg AFB in California could be more easily recovered in the shallow lagoon. Mini submarines were used for recovery purposes. Our project's radars were on Roi-Namur Island, on the other end of the lagoon. The bachelors lived on Roi-Namur with the married personnel commuting by airplane every day from Kwajalien. The airplanes were ancient DC-3's and DC-4's. The warm, humid air and the vibration of the airplane would put you to sleep almost immediately. You could always tell the new people on the DC-3's as we sat on parallel benches on either side of the plane, facing each other. Until the plane took off the air would be stifling and required some getting used to. The new people usually turned slightly green until we got airborne. I was allowed to live on Kwajalien and commute to work with the married personnel. I tried living on Roi-Namur, but amenities were limited, not to mention the absence of females. On Roi-Namur there are still the remains of the Japanese WW II fortifications, including the admiral's house, concrete pillboxes, and a field artillery piece. One day a WWII bomb exploded under what was a hobby shop. Fortunately, no one was in the building at the time. Roi-Namur is actually two islands joined together by a causeway. Most of one island is jungle. There are the remains of a US landing craft on the next island down the atoll; the driver must have invaded the wrong island. The third island down the atoll from Roi-Namur had a small Marshallese settlement. The Japanese, who controlled the atoll from after WW I until the US invasion in WWII, had built a railroad from Roi-Namur to the third island, the remains of which were still visible. At low tide you could walk from Roi-Namur to the native island.

On Kwajalien there were about 5,000 people on an island that is ½ miles wide by 2½ miles long. About half of the island is taken up by the airport and golf course. The men wore Bermuda shorts to work and on evening social occasions would add long socks. The women would wear most anything, but muumuus were popular.

Six months of the year is the dry season, which had near perfect weather. The temperature varied about between 65 and the high 70's with low humidity. The wet season was hotter and more humid and took some getting used to, but the nights were always very pleasant. The Marshallese live on the neighboring island and commuted to jobs on Kwajalien by ferry. Some of the Marshallese were part Japanese, which made the women much better looking. It would have been nice if the test site had been in Polynesia where the natives are considerably better looking than the Marshallese.

In a short time on Kwajalien I was able to finish paying off my sister, who had lent me money to go to college, and to help my mother, who was unable to work for a few months, because of health problems. I would continue to loan money to my sister Lois until she got her Ph. D. in French literature as pay back for helping me to survive in college. It was also a good feeling to be socking away money for a rainy day.

Our R&D radars were highly sophisticated and were constantly being upgraded. Our radar building was three stories high with a 90-foot diameter antenna on the roof. The staffs of both Lincoln Labs and RCA had numerous Ph. Ds. It wasn't clear why so many high-powered technical people were needed. The RCA Service Company operated and maintained the radars. On occasion a scientific type individual would appear and request a series of measurements to be made. He would then publish the results in the form of a technical paper not giving the engineer would did all the measurements any credit. Our receiving system was complex, and I recall spending a great deal of time explaining to some of the technical gurus how the system worked. One technical paper was copied verbatim from an article in a microwave magazine. One of the Lincoln Lab chiefs asked me what I thought of the locally generated paper. I had to inform him where the info came from.

One mission night I came back to my work area to find a bunch of scientist types and Ph. Ds. grouped around a new radar receiver holding wrenches, which was truly frightening. Normally, when there is a problem in a work area, the responsible engineer is paged to look into the problem. After inquiring as to what the problem was, I unscrewed the coaxial cable to the receiver and noticed that the center pin was recessed. This could make the radar return signal intermittent. I replaced the cable and asked them to see if the problem went away, which it did. There seems to be a tendency among those technical people, who have limited hardware experience, to want to redesign the equipment when there is a problem. Equipment design is rarely the problem if something initially worked.

On mission days after our extensive system calibration procedures were completed, we would sit around, drink coffee, and swap tales while we waited for the missile launch from Vandenberg AFB. One such tale involved the radar installation at Thule, Greenland where several RCA engineers had worked, as told by the engineer who had been the night shift Operations Director at Thule. One night a radar return indicated that the Soviets had launched a missile directed at the US. President Eisenhower was roused from his bed and informed of the event. He ordered our nuclear forces to go on Red Alert and, as soon as a nuclear hit on a US target was confirmed, retaliate. This involved having the SAC bombers sitting on the ends of the runways ready to take off. No doubt the Russians, if they were on the ball, would be monitoring this activity. It turns out that the radar at Thule was so powerful that a radar return was received from the moon, which was mistaken for an incoming missile. Oh well, live and learn.

One day on the bulletin board there was a news article from the Huntsville, Alabama newspaper. Huntsville is the home of the Army Missile Command. The article stated that on a recent mission two objects were observed on either side of the missile shortly after liftoff by the many radars that track the missile across the Pacific, as the missile raced at several thousand miles per hour toward the Kwajalien atoll. Just before the missile re-entered the earth's atmosphere, the two objects peeled off. Now that is an interesting story for all the UFO deniers out there.

Basketball was very popular on Kwajalien at that time, and our project had some excellent players including a 6' 8" center and 6' 4" power forward, who had both played major college ball. We had five strong players and then there was me. I was the sixth man; we normally played a six-man rotation. I wasn't even on a high school team, but played a lot of schoolyard basketball. There was a lot of money bet on the games. Where else could you spend it? Under these circumstances you didn't want to screw up. We were probably the third best team on the island. One team even had a small college All-American player. During one game a teammate and I were on a fast break when I heard the opponent's center thundering down the court after us. He was 6' 5" and build like a tank and in general was an angry person. The story was that he had gunned down his wife in the Honolulu airport; there were a lot of workers from Hawaii on island. It was a good time to share the basketball. My teammate, who was bigger and about 40 pounds heavier than I was, liked to score. I passed the ball off and my teammate was knocked into the third row when he went in for the lay-up. Had it been me, it would have probably broken every bone in my body. One more basketball story, we were playing the best team on the island and were ahead by one point with time running out. The opponents were on a fast break and our 6' 4" forward and myself were defending. He takes the 5' 10" player leaving me with the 6' 2" guy who just happened to be a deadly shooter. I am 5' 10". When the deadly shooter goes up for a close range jump shot, just as he was about to release the ball I yelled, "blow it." It must have startled him as he missed the shot.

Bridge was also popular on the island, centered on a duplicate bridge club with yours truly as the bridge director, who runs the game. Word was out that a "hired gun" had arrived on island and was a Life Master. I was one of the better players on island and was sitting at the officers club bar one night waiting for the free movie to start next door. In walks an older gentleman who surveys the room. I knew it was the hired gun. He came directly over to my table and said, "Are you Linder?" I said, "Are you Swanson?" We spared around like a couple of gun fighters, seeing what we were up against. We later became bridge partners.

Later on I teamed up with a bridge partner who used to hang out at the officers club bar and would challenge anyone to a game of bridge for ANY amount of money. I would get a call at maybe 10 at night saying we've got some live ones. He said he would cover any losses. Having played duplicate bridge in Dallas, I knew there were some very good bridge players out there. Oddly enough, we never won or lost much money.

Poker was also very popular. For a while I played in a $20 limit game which in those days was a lot of money, still is for that matter. Although I did well, the $100 or $150 I usually won was simply not worth losing most of a night's sleep. It usually took about six hands to determine, if I were playing out of my league, at which point I would drop out of the game if overmatched.

Many of the engineers that I worked with were very serious stock market players. They subscribed to investment newsletters, stock chart services, etc. Through the years I was to learn that playing the market was a very high-risk venture.

There was a saying on the islands, "Don't get hurt and don't get sick." Although there were doctors and a hospital on Kwajalien, high quality medical help was 2000 miles away in Honolulu.

Going to Honolulu every six months was good R&R. The flight to Hawaii was by a prop DC-6, which took nine hours to go the 2000 miles. The flight was first class in that the food and service were excellent. Drinks were 25 cents. I would hang out at Waikiki. For my annual leave I turned in airline tickets in Hawaii for a trip to the Far East. Two of my friends and I went on a tour of the Orient. One friend, who was Hawaiian, was friends with a Japanese women that now lived in Tokyo. We arranged to meet her in a bar. As the evening wore on an attractive young Japanese girl came by our table and our Japanese lady friend explained that the girl was a "business girl" in case we were interested. For a fairly nominal price she could be available for an all night rendezvous. At that time I was used to dating women in the States, taking them to dinner, etc., and often managing to get a goodnight kiss, if I was lucky. This was a whole new ballgame. We spent a very enjoyable night together.

The three of us decided to take a tour of Japan. At some out of the way place, where we stopped for the night, the motel manager wanted to know if we wanted to go bowling. It was a very quiet place so two of us said why not. As we were bowling, a crowd began to gather. I was not a great bowler, maybe carrying a 135-140 average and my friend was at 150 plus. When we would strike or spare, the crowd would cheer. The alleys had apparently just opened, and the Japanese had not quite got the hang of the game. It was fun to be a bowling star, even if it was not justified. At our Kyoto stop we were at a nightclub, and I asked this very attractive Japanese girl to dance. As it turns out she was a "business girl." After negotiating the price, we went to a Japanese style motel and spent the night. She even escorted me by taxi back to my hotel. Again, as in Tokyo, it was a very pleasant experience.

My two friends were flying on a US military plane and on the Taiwan leg of our trip had arrived there ahead of me. When I deplaned in Taipei, there was a huge banner reading, "Welcome Bruce Linder." A "guide" meets me and explained that my friends were staying at a hotel in the resort area of Peitou. The deal was that you could have three girls per day, a room with an attached sitting room, and meals. Three a day was a little too much, so I settled for the two-a-day plan after a couple of days. Japanese businessmen would come to the hotel for sex parties and the lobby in the evening would be full of young ladies. I would often go through the lobby with my "guide" and select my date for that night. The girls were not very fond of the sex parties; they said the Japanese businessmen wanted to do all kinds of kinky things. One night after I selected my date for the night, my "guide" said, "no, no you don't want her; she hasn't been to school." It turns out he was talking about sex school.

One of my friends would buy expensive bottles of booze at the military PX, where we had privileges, and give it to the maids in an attempt to seduce them, although he was paying for sex twice a day. Go figure.

On the Taiwan/Hong Kong leg of our trip I met a Chinese girl who worked in NYC. She showed me around Hong Kong. We would go to some large nightclub with her relatives where I would be the only Caucasian in the place. It was a strange experience.

As you might guess, on a small, rather boring island, where people don't wear much clothing, there were indiscretions. When a couple, who were not married to each other, were found on the beach, golf course, or any place outside of their quarters in an inappropriate situation; the persons involved and their spouses, if any, were shipped off the island. The Northwest Airline planes that they left on had a red tail, hence the name of being "red-tailed out." It happened more often than you would think.

After a couple of years on Kwajalien of soaking up money, it was time to move on. Living and working on tiny islands gets to you after awhile. Now that I had a taste of making a lot more money and working on interesting projects, I wanted to work overseas. Sitting in an office working with a bunch of technical people in the States wasn't really that rewarding or exciting. RCA had a job in Germany so it was back to Boston to train on a missile system for army tanks. It turns out that the European tank commander didn't want the missile system on his tanks because the enemy tank could turn and fire its cannon before the missile you had just fired got there.

CHAPTER 6

STATESIDE

RCA TALKED ME into taking a job in Santa Barbara monitoring the development of multilayer circuit cards to be used in landing radar computer of the lunar excursion module (LEM) of the space program. It was easy work because I was dating an assembly girl, and she told me everything that went on. There was also per diem, overtime pay, and a car thrown in so I could bank my paycheck. Santa Barbara was quite a change from Boston. People were friendly, somewhat laid back and courteous drivers. It was somewhat amazing that drivers at a four way stop during rush hour would take their turns; try that in Boston, where there was no such thing as the right of way. In Boston if you didn't have a local accent, you were often not well received. Maybe it's those narrow two lane roads that they have or the weather that irritates them; who knows.

It was very noticeable that in Santa Barbara people did not think of themselves as being old. In Boston and New Jersey you would see women in there 50's hunched over in their long black coats in winter, saying to the world, my children have left home and I'm old now.

The circuit board manufacturer, to prevent RCA from finding out all the problems, limited me to two, ten minute escorted tours of their facility a day. It didn't matter, as my girl friend kept me clued in. On occasion I would have to fly back to Boston for meetings. On return-ing to Santa Barbara at night it seems it was often very foggy on the trip from LAX. Leaving the San Fernando Valley, I would get behind a large truck and follow it all the way to Santa Barbara; there were some really reckless drivers out there.

Finally, I recommended that RCA shut the production down, as the vendor would never produce a usable product. Maybe that wasn't such a good idea, because I was sent to New Hampshire and Camden, New Jersey in January to monitor other vendors. When I went to Camden, I was booked into a downtown hotel near work. It doesn't take a rocket scientist to realize Camden is a very dangerous place. A federal judge was mugged in the restroom of my hotel at lunchtime. The next night it was out to the Cherry Hill Inn, which is next door to the RCA Service Company headquarters.

RCA couldn't come up with anything interesting overseas so I hired into Sylvania in the Boston area on the promise of jobs in South America and Europe. One of my first tasks was to review the pricing that another engineer had done for a proposal of a communications system in Guyana. It was clear that management didn't like the engineer, and I was encouraged to find that his efforts were unsatisfactory. A meeting was called, and I was put on the spot to critique his work. Much to the displeasure of management, I found no fault with his effort. Throughout my engineering career I had to point out to my management at times, that I was hired to be an honest engineer. If they wanted me to be dishonest, they would have to pay me a lot more money.

No overseas jobs materialized, and after hanging around for several weeks with nothing to do, I was getting nervous. So, I walked into the office next door and asked, "What do you guys do here and do you need any engineers?"

Once again fate intervenes:

The response was that they were looking for a microwave engineer to go to Chile ASAP to work on the installation of a satellite interfacing earth station. My response was, "I'm a microwave engineer."

CHAPTER 7

CHILE

TWO DAYS LATER I landed in Santiago, Chile after a 24-hour turbo-jet flight from Miami. My right arm was swollen up twice its normal size from a reaction to a typhoid shot given to me by the company doctor. At the airport I was met by two young men, who didn't speak any English, and unfortunately, I took German in school. I couldn't go crash, but had to go out to the site to meet the boss for some strange reason.

At my motel in Santo Domingo de Rocas, which was on the ocean, for breakfast the next morning I got a cold ham and cheese sandwich. The waiter didn't speak any English and of course the menu was in Spanish. This is not going well. But aha! The next morning things were different. I ordered ham and eggs, toast, coffee, and orange juice in Spanish. I think that the waiter the previous morning was just being a jerk. I foolishly assumed that Chile, being close to Brazil, would have really good coffee. Due to import restrictions the only coffee was instant Nescafe. That is really cruel. On the plus side Chile had good beer and some inexpensive, really excellent wines. The climate is very similar to southern California. One nice thing about working in Chile was that you could exchange your paycheck on the black market for about double the official exchange rate. Prices were already low compared with the US, but now even lower.

There was no help in finding a place to live. Everyone seemed to be staying in Santo Domingo de Rocas. I was informed that certain members of the installation team had rented a large house there and were allowing their local girl friends to stay there. It was clear management did not approve. Fortunately, they had an open bedroom so I moved in. Santo Domingo de Rocas is a summertime resort town on the ocean. Since it was wintertime, rents were very cheap. The only problem to this arrangement was that the guys wanted to go to the nightclub in the nearby seaport city of San Antonio almost every night. The guys that didn't have a live-in girl friend would often bring a pro home with them. We were working 60 hours a week. What the hell, I was in my late 20's and some of the guys were in there 40's so I should be able to keep up with them. In those days it cost five dollars to hire a girl for all night. Even then, five dollars was not much money.

During my career working overseas, I would run into American men, who would brag that they never paid for sex. I would patiently explain to them, that by wining and dining the local gals, they were paying far more than if they had simply negotiated a price for the evening activities. Also, you could just relax, knowing how the evening was going to turn out.

The professional girls in Chile would have health inspections every week, and if there were any questions; they would whip out their dated inspection slip. I don't recall ever having a bad experience, when I hired a girl for the evening. Well, each to his own.

Along with the house that we rented came a cook/maid and her husband, who was the gardener. They lived in a cottage on the property. Since no one else was trying to learn Spanish, I was designated to be the interface. Very few people in Chile spoke any English. Two of the live-in girl friends helped with the menu planning. One of the girl friends spoke some German so we communicated in German. Some nights when I arrived at the dinner table, there would be no Americans there. Some of the dinner guests I had never seen before. One such guest was the local butcher. There were only a few days a week that you could order beef in the restaurants, and it usually wasn't that great. He was a great guest as he provided really good steaks, which we had difficulty buying in the market.

One of my work assignments was to go to a microwave relay station, which was on a very high, steep hill. There was a narrow dirt road that wound its way to the top of the hill with a sheer drop off of a few hundred feet on one side. Fortunately, the country was in a severe drought. Transiting that road was scary enough without any rain or mud. The testing was long and boring so one night, when I had to go to the relay station; I stopped by the house and got a bottle of wine and one of the live-in girl friends. The wine and the company helped to keep things warm on a very cold night. The view was spectacular. Mount Aconcogua, the highest peak in the Western Hemisphere, could be seen. No electric lights were visible in any direction.

Many strange and unusual things happened in Chile. Part of the reason is that you don't speak the language well and the culture is different. It was not unusual to meet nice looking, young women just hanging around or hitch hiking. A fellow worker and I decided to rent an apartment in Santiago, because the nightlife in Santo Domingo de Rocas was nonexistent. Our nasty technical manager would not allow us to use a company vehicle so we rented a little rattletrap. One night while driving through a farm town on the way to Santiago, there were two nice looking young ladies standing on a street corner. I told my friend to drive around the block. We pulled over and asked them if they wanted to go to Santiago. They spent the night at our apartment and my friend who was the Spanish speaker gave them bus fare back home the next morning. I recalled the many nights of unsuccessfully trying to pick up women in the States. The women in Chile were much more interested in sex than women in the States. Several of the guys, who seemed to be confirmed bachelors, got married while in Chile.

One night in Santiago, I found myself sitting in a nightclub with two friends from work and three local girls. I can honestly say that they were three of the best-looking girls that I had ever seen. Out of boredom, while working in Santa Barbara, I took dance lessons at a local dance studio. We did a lot of cha-cha-cha, but I never really had an opportunity to make use of the lessons. Through my somewhat alcohol fogged brain, I realized that the band was playing a cha-cha-cha. My date and I had the whole dance floor to ourselves. She didn't know some of the steps, but she faked it well.

There was a very popular nightclub on the outskirts of Santiago called the, "Las Tres Brujas," which is, "The Three Witches," in English. The place was pitch black so when you were dancing, there was no fear of any embarrassment. They were playing a lot of rock and roll, and my date and I were out there gyrating with the best of them. The locals were somewhat impressed with our dancing and cleared part of the dance floor for us. They said that was pretty good for Chile. They asked if I was in the Peace Corp. We got that often, and probably gave the Peace Corp a bad name with all the carousing around that we did.

The police in Santiago had a cute trick of towing away our cars at night. We had big blue station wagons with New York plates. No other cars parked near us would be towed. I think it was $10 to get the car back the next day. I called the US Embassy about the problem; good luck if you ever need help overseas.

Some of the more bizarre stories were:

I was paired to work nights with an engineer who had been teaching the Chilenos about the system in the States, and he was also fairly fluent in Spanish. After having had a few drinks at dinner one night, when we arrived at site, my fellow engineer began berating the Chileno trainees in Spanish; why, I had no idea. The next day he was gone and yours truly, the newest, least knowledgeable person on site was left alone at night to run the now operational satellite station. It seemed that every night about 3:00AM, all hell would break loose. Alarm bells, flashing red lights, etc. I had uncovered where some of the Chileno trainees, who were supposed to be helping, slept. I would roust them out and together we would try to fix the problem. One night at about 3:00 AM, of course, I get this frantic call from Fucino, Italy, which was the master satellite control station. I am trying to understand his Spanish with my very limited knowledge of the language. Finally, I tried English, which he spoke fluently. He probably wondered why my English was so much better than my Spanish. By some miracle the station never went down. Our technical manager had commandeered on-site living quarters for him and his wife and would sneak in at all hours of the night to see if he could catch me sleeping on the job, an unusual fellow. Strange that he was never around when there were problems, and he never volunteered his help. He also tried to enlist me to go to rallies for the "oppressed workers" of the fundos (large farms). Not a healthy thing to do in those days.

Working the night shift alone was not all bad. When I got home I would sit in front of a huge stone fireplace in the living room, which always seemed to have a roaring fire going in it and have a glass of wine. There would always be one or two live-in girl friends sitting around; I would teach them to say outrageous things to their boy friends in English like "Next to your paycheck, I like you the best." Sometimes one of the pros that were there from the night before would surprise me by jumping in bed with me.

On my way to work at night, I would sometimes stop at a tiny restaurant/bar in a cluster of houses in the absolute middle of nowhere to get a ham sandwich and a bottle of wine for my mid-shift snack. There, one night on a barstool sat our site administrative manger. Sensing something must be wrong, I hung around and sure enough, he confided that he had not slept with his wife in three months, yet she was pregnant. The best that I could do was to blurt out, "It sounds like an immaculate conception." Later, the story was that the local bus driver was the guilty party.

One more story about the manager's wife. Early one morning the door to my bedroom was flung open and a black haired, rather dark skinned woman was standing there with her hands on her hips. I assumed that she was a local Chilena. In bed with me was a young lady, who I had brought home from the nightclub the night before. My response to this intrusion was to say, "You will have to wait your turn." At the time I didn't know who she was. It seems that she was there to commandeer a company vehicle to go shopping, which was very much against the rules.

When I would be working with hand tools, I would lay one down to go get something. When I returned, it had disappeared. I recruited the biggest, meanest looking local employee to be my hand tool manager and spread the word that, if any more hand tools went missing, Carlos would break someone's arm. After that, no more tools disappeared.

The satellite ground station was now ready to be turned over to the Chilean government. A lavish party was held at site with the President of Chile, Eduardo Frei, and the Catholic Bishop of Santiago in attendance. After listening to several speeches of various people taking credit for the completion of the installation and testing of the system, I spotted a cute, young, female newspaper reporter who looked as bored as I was. After a brief conversation, I grabbed a bottle of champagne and took her on a private tour of the facility. I don't know if the tour made it into her news report or not. Many years later I ran into a couple from Chile in Waikiki and mentioned I had worked in their country when Eduardo Frei was President. They said that his son, Eduardo Frei Jr., was the current president, interesting.

At the time I was leaving Chile, there was a three-way presidential election campaign going on among two conservatives and a Communist, Salvador Allende. Allende won with just slightly more than one third of the vote. The election was hailed in the US press as a victory for socialism, failing to mention that the conservatives polled almost two thirds of the vote. About 18 months later, while working in Brazil, I had the opportunity to return briefly to Santiago. I asked the local GTE office mangers how the new president was working out. They said that he had shut down Santiago's largest newspaper because it was critical of his policies, and that high-ranking military officers were being assassinated. From my brief stay in Chile I got the impression that the police and military were tough, no nonsense organizations, and that they would not tolerate Allende much longer.

I was not surprised to read that he was removed from office, which horrified the US press. No mention was ever made in the US of what had been going on during his reign.

One thing that was noticeable in Chile was that news stories in the local papers presented the news from the US straight up, no slant, no political bias. Later, I found this to also be true in Brazil, Pakistan, and Saudi Arabia.

CHAPTER **8**

PAKISTAN

MY NEXT ASSIGNMENT after Chile was Pakistan. Surprisingly, two of the people that I worked with in Chile had spent time in Pakistan and their descriptions did not sound promising. I thought; it can't possibly be that bad. It was. Comparatively, Chile was heaven, and Pakistan was hell.

On returning to the States I had the opportunity to check out two possible retirement locations that had been highly recommended. At age 29 I was already thinking about not working. The first was San Jose, Costa Rica. It was a long bus ride from the airport through green, rolling hills to San Jose. The town reminded me of a not overly prosperous town in Mexico. The people on the street were not well dressed. From my hotel room it looked like a lot of stores on the main street had tin roofs. On a tour of the city I asked to see the nicest housing area. At best it would be considered middle class in the States. They did have really good coffee and an opera house, however.

While working on Kwajalien several people talked about investing money in Mexico through an American living in Monterey, Mexico. The yield was good, and it was allegedly a very safe investment. I stopped in Monterey to check it out. That night the American, probably in his early sixties, suggested we go to a house of ill repute. As we were selecting our dates for the night, he asked how much cash I had on me. It was a couple of hundred dollars. He said that we could easily be killed for that amount of money. I did invest some money with him and it turned out well.

As part of my preparation for the Pakistan adventure, I was sent to Redwood City, California for two weeks to train on the microwave radio equipment that I was to teach the Pakistanis. There was only one of the two radio types available so I would have to fake it somewhat, when I got to Pakistan.

On the way across country I stopped by South Dakota to visit my mother and brother, Brian. Their TV set was so bad, that it looked liked ghosts moving across the screen instead of people. I wrote a check for a good TV set. Whenever I was in town, I would take my mother grocery shopping and tell her to buy everything that she could possibly think of. I got in the habit of sending her substantial checks for Easter, Christmas, and her birthday. Wages in Brookings were pathetic.

The second highly recommended retirement spot was Las Palmas in the Canary Islands. The job in Pakistan was delayed, so I told my management at Sylvania to contact me in Las Palmas. To keep your federal tax-free status you had to limit the number of days in the US during any 18-month period. I wound up spending four weeks soaking up the sun. The weather was great, but the place seemed to be a poor man's Hawaii. Unlike Hawaii there appeared to be very little rainfall, which made things very dry and barren.

On to Karachi: For kicks I got routed through Moscow. At the Moscow airport there was only one plane sitting on the ground, an ancient turbo prop of the Polish Airlines. When we deplaned, there were two soldiers with submachine guns at the bottom of the stairs that took our passports. The terminal was huge with gigantic propaganda posters extolling the workers' paradise. I was the only human roaming around this mammoth terminal. No planes arrived or departed, no kiosks, very spooky.

On departing the same two guards were returning passports after carefully matching pictures with the departing passengers. I guess they didn't want any citizens of the workers' paradise sneaking out of the country. On boarding there was also a soldier with a submachine gun monitoring the cabin cleanup crew.

On arriving in Karachi I was supposed to be met at the airport by our local representative, who did not appear. Somehow I was not surprised. I grabbed a taxi to the best hotel in town, the Intercontinental, which was the only westernized hotel. There was no reservation in my name. The phones did work there unlike at the airport, and the local rep informed me that my hotel was just across the street. Before I left for Pakistan, the GTE International and Sylvania managers said, if I had problems in Pakistan, don't tell them because they didn't want to know. That was just fine with me as I enjoyed working alone and being completely independent.

I would now begin a strange and often bizarre 10 and 1/2 months in Pakistan. Before the first class started, the head of the PT&T training department informed me that the books and radio equipment were being held up at the docks by the longshoremen, who wanted a bribe to release them. After consulting with GTE International in New York, I informed him that no bribes would be paid by GTE to ransom the training material. I would meet daily with the training department guru, and eventually the material got to the training school. Going from my hotel to the training department offices involved stop and go driving through a large leper colony in downtown Karachi. That was quite an experience.

The first class of students was supposed to be unfamiliar with electronics, and I would bring them up to speed and then teach them the operation and maintenance of a microwave communications system, which was being installed in East Pakistan, now Bangladesh. Much to my surprise, this class consisted of college-degreed engineers who were presently maintaining a microwave radio system. Fortunately, the classes only lasted six hours a day giving me time to go back to my hotel and study like hell to stay ahead of them.

Teaching a class of 40 young Pakistanis was an exercise in control. I used a "pointer" that was actually a large, round, thick stick. It is not easy to argue with or confront someone waving a big club around. All went well.

40

It was pointed out to me by one of my assistant instructors that it cost $15 to have someone killed in Karachi, if you were important; but only $10 if the person was no one special. This conversation came about because I was working the students fairly hard by Pakistani standards. It was suggested that I ease off a little. I figured that I was probably a $10 hit. Easing off seemed like a good idea.

When the first class was nearing completion, the head of the training school suggested that he might delay the start of the second class, if I wanted go to Bangkok, sin city of the world, to get my batteries recharged, a brilliant idea. Payback I found out later was to allow his son to attend the next training class, and to see if I could get him a job oh the microwave relay installation project in East Pakistan. It turns out his son was bright and a nice guy. Now I am catching on to the way things work in Pakistan. I packed a suitcase with things of limited value and asked the hotel to store it for me, "forgetting" to put a nametag on it.

On the way into town from the Bangkok airport I asked the cab driver if it would be possible to have a social engagement prior to going to my hotel. He watched my luggage while a got my batteries recharged. In Karachi there weren't many women around period. In Bangkok I stayed in a good western style hotel. I had my first steak and green salad in over four months, fantastic. Then on to the hotel nightclub where a sexy young French woman was singing in French while I sipped cognac. From hell it was back to heaven. A nice feature in Bangkok was the massage parlors. The massage girls sat behind a glass partition with numbers on their blouses so you could select the girl you wanted. You could have a beer and get a very good massage. I let the girl walk on my back as part of the massage, which felt great. If you wanted to arrange a social engagement for later, the prices were at a fixed rate. In Bangkok it was hard to avoid sex if you were by yourself. One night before going out I stopped at the hotel bar for a drink and immediately two young Thai ladies sat down on either side of me and very aggressively explained what they would like to do for me. There was a well-known coffee shop called the "Na Na," which was populated wall to wall with young Thai women. I have never been anywhere, where sex was so easily available.

On returning to Karachi via Dacca in East Pakistan I met a nice young American husband and wife Christian missionary team on their way up country. And I thought my assignment was challenging. The Pakistan International Airways (PIA) flight to Karachi was scary. We were in a typhoon that went on and on. It was the only time that I had been really concerned for my safety in an airplane. An Air India plane did go down in that storm. On returning to my hotel in Karachi, surprise, surprise, my suitcase was missing. Since the hotel was run by the two airlines, KLM and PIA, they had to reimburse me for lost luggage. Score one for the good guys.

The American in charge of the microwave relay system installation in East Pakistan was in town and at dinner he asked how would he find a young lady for the evening. It never crossed my mind to investigate on my own, as it didn't seem like a good idea in a Moslem country, but what the heck. Cab drivers know everything, so here we are in this very dark and somewhat scary part of town. Two girls got in the cab and sat on the floor. We pulled up to the back of a motel and went up the back stairs. The intrigue made things more interesting.

I had the opportunity to go to a dentist. His equipment looked like it belonged in a dental museum, but it was several cuts above the street dentists, who worked on their patients while both the dentist and the patient sat on their haunches on the sidewalk.

Things were beginning to get a bit dicey in Karachi. There was a lot of unrest as the people were unhappy with their military officer President, Ayub Khan. One of my forms of entertainment was to take a taxi downtown to buy a Herald Tribune newspaper at the Intercontinental Hotel. The trip into town was through a series of small towns dotting the semi-desert landscape. There were two patches of green grass in Karachi, both of which were always shown in the tourist brochures, yes, "tourist brochures." At my hotel the front desk sent a young women to my room one day to help the tourist bureau come up with something to lure tourists to Karachi. She had lived in New

York City. It was quite a conversation, and we didn't part agreeing on the charms of Karachi.

Sometimes while waiting for a taxi to go back to my hotel, lepers from the downtown leper colony would try to touch me while begging for money. I would sometimes swat them with my newspaper to drive them off. I had tried to connect with other Americans at the US Consulate, but that was a dead end. They were even evasive as to where the 4th of July picnic was being held. There were two British engineers staying at the hotel who were supervising the repair of a British Airways plane that had been shot up at the Karachi Airport by some terrorist group. We bonded as the only westerners at the hotel. I lived within running distance to the airport. I also had an open airline ticket in case I needed to bail out in a hurry.

Occasionally, an American would show up for breakfast at the hotel. I would introduce myself, sit down and mention that if some local gave them a special suitcase to smuggle drugs or money out of the country, their Pakistani friend had already called customs to let them know that suitcase #xyz would be coming through. From the startled looks on the faces of some of them, I probably saved them some serious jail time. The game, of course, was to elicit a bribe to spring the poor devil from jail. One morning at breakfast I ran into a Dutchman who was in Pakistan putting in a dairy. He was quite proud of the fact that he had invented a tamper proof milk carton. The Pakistani milk delivery drivers were stealing the milk and replacing it with chalk and water.

It dawned on me that my letters to the States were not getting through. To solve the problem I would send the letters registered and insist on having the postal employee cancel the stamps, when I mailed them. The postal employees had been pealing the stamps off and throwing the letters away.

The head of the training school invited me to go to the horse races with him one day. On the first race he bet the equivalent of one year's salary and lost! This incident would explain some later events.

Since the next class contained the students that were supposed to have been in the first class, I needed very little preparation time. These students had no knowledge of electronics. Going into town was not that enjoyable. I would usually attract a small crowd of people wanting to sell me drugs, be my guide, etc. Often women beggars would come up to me and put their hand in my face and say, "You give me rupees!" You learn to say no in a hurry. Visiting GTE International personnel sometimes would run down the street so that they could give money to a beggar, thanks a lot.

Now fate intervenes once more:

Out of a clear blue sky my brother Julian sends me a book on yoga. Since I had nothing else to do, I would spend 2-3 hours a day doing exercises and then go swimming. People would remark on how healthy I looked. I learned much later that many yoga instructors do not teach the headstand, which is called the king of asanas (exercises). To me the headstand is by far the best yoga pose. Yoga is great for travelers; you can do it in your hotel room. It has great recuperative powers, especially the headstand and backward bending. No doubt any series of exercises would be beneficial. I went with my students on a field trip to the ancient ruins of Moenjadaro near the Indus River. Little did I know then that 5,000 year-old statuettes were found of people doing yoga poses.

On general strike days, you were not supposed to be out and about. Coming home from downtown one general strike day while my taxi was going through a small town, a mob threw rocks at the cab. One particularly large one bounced on the pavement and rolled across the hood of the taxi. The driver was not fazed, but after that I tended to stay close to the hotel on strike days. One strike day I went to the training school to see what was going on. The school was very close to my hotel. Stepping into a large courtyard area, I saw a large, angry crowd of students. In there midst was the head of the training school. I started to walk backward very slowly hoping not to be spotted. But, alas, the head of the training school spots me and yells, "Mr. Linder, Mr. Linder!" The crowd parts and we engage in a detailed and meaningless discussion about my lesson plans, as if we were not surrounded by an angry mob. Suddenly, the training school head looks around as if he had just noticed the mob and says, "You can gather here, but there will be no shouting of slogans." He turns and walks right at the mob. If the crowd parts we will probably live, if not, well, you would probably not be reading this. Just like the Israelites at the Red Sea, a pathway was made for him.

Later, I learned that he was extorting money from each student who came to the training school. Earlier, when our microwave radios arrived, he informed me that there was a problem. He had already been paid for installing them and didn't know how to handle the situation. I came in nights with the East Pakistani students, who weren't overly fond of the West Pakistanis, to install the radios. I later heard that someone threw a hand grenade into his living room. Fortunately, no one was injured.

The houseboys at my hotel would get upset, when I would leave the door to my room open. They would go in my room and spray for mosquitoes. I later read in the newspaper that Karachi had the highest incidence of malaria in the world. I started taking anti-malaria pills, but gave them up when I read that they can lead to blindness. Karachi also had a high rate of cholera, but that doesn't sound good, so they called it gastroenteritis, aka stomach flu. One of my students claimed that he got typhoid from drinking bottled soda. Many times during my stay I thought about packing up and leaving, but I guess stubbornness or pride got the better of me. I was getting a 25% bonus plus per diem and a few hours of overtime pay, but you could get that much working just about anywhere overseas.

In defense of the Pakistanis, I must say that I was treated well. When I would be waiting for a taxi, I would often be offered rides by well meaning drivers. They were also excellent bridge players and a few times the head of the training school and two of his engineers from the training department and I played bridge in my hotel's lounge area.

With about two weeks left in my teaching assignment, the head of the training school calls me into his office and says, "I have some very good news." Hmmm, maybe I get out of jail early. "At great expense to the government of Pakistan, we are extending your stay by six weeks." It was like getting a serious blow to your midsection.

When I arrived in Karachi, for some reason GTE International wasn't sending my expense checks despite numerous phone calls and telegrams on my part. I had been converting dollars into rupees at the official rate knowing it would be a real pain in the rear end trying to repatriate the rupees back to dollars. Later, I learned that I could do the conversion on the black market, where the rate was double the official rate. My bank in Boston had been taking money out of my checking account instead of putting money in, causing my black market checks to bounce. Fortunately, the black market trader was very understanding, and we got it straightened out. Armed with a stack of paperwork I tried to make the currency exchange when leaving the country. The official obviously wanted a bribe. The country was now under marshal law and an army lieutenant could sentence you to seven years in prison with no possibility of appeal. So I told the official that there was a marshal law administrator, i.e. army lieutenant, downstairs, and I would bring him up and let him settle it. He chickened out and gave me my dollars back.

When I was leaving Pakistan, the head of the PT&T training department, the head of the training school, and their wives took me out to dinner, which I thought was a very nice gesture.

ESCAPE FROM PAKISTAN

IN LEAVING PAKISTAN I was supposed to fly PIA, but flying KLM sounded a lot better. The PIA flights left at reasonable hours, but the KLM flight was around midnight. In the departure lounge they didn't announce foreign carrier flights so I went around asking people, who looked like seasoned travelers, if they were flying KLM. A shuttle bus pulled up unannounced, which was for the KLM flight. I landed in Zurich. The next morning was a Sunday. I went for a walk in a nearby park. It was a beautiful fall day. There was green grass, flowers, and clean, well-dressed people. It was hell back to heaven. The Swiss-German that they speak in Zurich was different than the German that I had studied in college and wasn't that easy to understand. I should have taken a third year of German instead of Russian; it might have helped. My next assignment would be in Brazil, but it wouldn't open up for awhile. After about one month in Zurich, I got a notice to appear at the local police station. They wanted to make sure that I was not working in Switzerland. To preserve my tax-free status, I hung out in Zurich until it started getting cold and then headed for London.

In Zurich and London I would spend time in the stockbrokers' offices watching the Dow-Jones trading tape. I was able to reinforce my belief that I could not accurately predict stock market prices.

I also started to study Portuguese and enlisted a nice looking Brazilian girl from the Brazilian Embassy to teach me. I was able to find a nice hotel near Kensington Gardens. There was some kind of housing for US military personnel near my hotel, and the area shop people were not overly friendly, which was unusual for London. For amusement I would select some stop on the underground and go there, walk around and have my mid-morning tea. It was fun giving the Brits directions on the underground. They would usually get a funny look on their faces, when they realized that a Yank was giving them directions. While in London I met a cute blonde at a night-club. She had just returned from the States and wasn't working, so she showed me around London.

In the London newspaper there was a story about an old church near where I was staying. When walking home from the underground stop a couple of days later, a car pulls up and someone asked me in German where the church was. To my surprise I was able to give him directions with my limited German. He probably thought everyone in London spoke German.

CHAPTER 10

BRAZIL

ONE EVENING I was in my London hotel room watching the snow falling in the park next door, when the phone rang. It was Boston calling. It was time to go to Brazil. I was to be the US representative to oversee the writing of a proposal to the State of Sao Paulo for a television microwave link system for the entire state. On the way back to Boston and New York to check in, I was requested to go to Milan, Italy and check out the microwave radios produced by a GTE subsidiary there. The Italians really know how to entertain. We went to a very nice restaurant and the locals ordered for me. For kicks I stopped off in Barcelona on the way back to Boston. In waking up the next morning to a ringing telephone, at first, I didn't know what country I was in or what language they were speaking. Having a couple of drinks the night before didn't help matters. Some down time back in the States was beginning to sound like a good idea.

On my arrival in Sao Paulo one of my first questions was, "Why is the proposal being written in English?" It wasn't. So, one of my first tasks was to be able to read Portuguese. After a few months in Sao Paulo and many Portuguese lessons later, if someone stopped me on the street to ask a question, they didn't realize that I wasn't a local, just a little slow. Having worked in Chile, I at least had some background as Spanish is similar to Portuguese. At the GTE office I told the Brazilians that I would only speak Portuguese while at work, which seemed to work out well.

One of the things that I was looking forward to was having some good Brazilian coffee, since they are a major coffee producer. Much to my disappointment the coffee was very strong and bitter, served in tiny cups, which you had to add a lot of sugar to. It took some getting used to. At dinner at my hotel I would have tomato soup as an appetizer. As my Portuguese got better, I realized that I could have six oysters on the half shell, which were really nice and fresh, cheaper than canned tomato soup. Some of my American friends at the hotel would drink scotch whiskey, which was very expensive. It turns out that there was a Brazilian made rum, which was very powerful, that you could get a water glass full for ten cents. It was an easy choice.

I had a favorite restaurant for lunch. One day I noticed that the most expensive item on the menu was tatu. The waiter couldn't explain was it was, but what the heck, it must be good. It tasted rather gamey and after consulting the dictionary that night, it turns out it was armadillo.

My passport was expiring so I went to the American Consulate to get a new one. Sitting behind the desk was a woman that lived in the same apartment house in Dallas that I did, and who I used to play duplicate bridge with. She had married a Brazilian. She got me into a group of Americans and Brazilians that played duplicate bridge, small world.

At my hotel in Sao Paulo I became friends with a black American, who was there long term. We would go to this raunchy nightclub. It helped to have a drink or two before hand as it seemed to be a gangster hangout and was in general a scary place. My friend preferred black girls, and when we arrived two or three would often stop at our table. These gals could best be described as rather exotic.

The GTE International executives from New York were in town. In a city of ten million people, who should we meet at noontime walking down the street, but one of my friend's girlfriends. She gave me a very friendly greeting and called me by name. No explaining that one.

At the hotel where I stayed there would often be a few mid-level Detroit auto company executives staying there for six weeks of training on how their Brazilian subsidiary assembly plants operated. They were for the most part not fun people. Some would want to know "Where are the girls?" My friend and I would take them to our favorite hangout. On sitting down two or three slinky-looking black girls would come over to our table. This seemed to unnerve the car company executives. One said that he was trying to get the attention of a nice looking blonde in a red dress, but she was ignoring him. I waved to her, shouted a few words in Portuguese; she came over and jumped on his lap. He suddenly had to go back to the hotel and write a letter to his wife. As you might guess, all the girls at the nightclub were pros. To hire a girl for all night cost ten dollars.

On a consulting trip back to the States I found out that I had a new manger at Sylvania. I explained to him that my previous boss had said that if the per diem rate for Sao Paulo was inadequate, that Sylvania would retroactively adjust it. Armed with hotel receipts, I presented my case. He wasn't interested in increasing the per diem rate retroactively, so I suggested that Sylvania send another engineer, who was knowledgeable in microwave radio communications systems and who could read Portuguese, back to Brazil in two days time. Suddenly, Sylvania found that they could readjust the per diem. It's nice to hold all the aces.

When sitting having a drink at our Sao Paulo hotel, my friend and I would have a soccer match on the radio, and when one of the car execs would appear, we would crank up the volume and listen intently, not having a clue as to what was being said. One fellow in particular was a pain in the rear end. There was a gay bar near our hotel, which was also known as an illegal drug distribution center. We told our new friend that it was our secret hangout, but we would let him in on it. He came back raving about how friendly all the guys were; they kept buying him drinks. This guy was not the brightest candle on the cake.

As we neared completion of our proposal, there was a meeting of my boss from New York, our local GTE International office manager (a retired Brazilian AF general), and the governor of the State of Sao Paulo, who was also a Brazilian AF general. The military was running Brazil at the time. We met at a TV studio where the general had just given a televised speech. The four of us sat side by side in the middle of a large room with the governor's 20 or so bodyguards ringing the room. The two generals were talking money, and because of the six months that I had been intensely studying Portuguese, I was picking up on their conversation. My take on the conversation was that they were discussing bribes, i.e., who got how much money. This was not healthy information to know about, so I did my best to look very bored by the conversation. Two days later the lead story in Sao Paulo's largest newspaper was that GTE International was to get a no bid contract with the State of Sao Paulo. The next day I got a call from New York saying that the party was over.

My next assignment was to be a two-year assignment in Rio to try to sell educational electronics to government schools. Two years in Rio sounded like a fun assignment. Unfortunately, my GTE International boss in New York got sacked, and I was told to come home.

Carnival in Rio was in full swing so on my way back to Boston, I spent four days in Rio. Carnival in Rio has to be experienced, to be believed. It was a nonstop party. I didn't sleep for three nights. No one questioned my expenses for four days in Rio. Contrary to popular belief, the girls on the beaches in Rio are not all that beautiful. At Ipanema I saw very few really nice looking women. I did find a girl friend though, which was easy to do during Carnival. The GTE International offices in Rio were right on the parade route so I had an excellent view of the festivities.

CHAPTER 11

TEACHING SEMINARS

THE ONLY JOB of interest back at Sylvania in Boston was teaching seminars in Communications. Amazingly, I saw an ad for a furnished apartment for rent by the month. I immediately called and said I would take it. By the time I got to the apartment house two other people had already called. It was even close to work. My apartment was right next to Brandeis University in Waltham. When driving home there were often Brandeis students hitch hiking from the main bus route back to their campus, a couple of miles away. I always stopped and offered them a ride, since it was easy to pull into the school's semi-circular drive to let them off. It was strange that they were never very friendly or appreciative; maybe it was a stressful school.

From my technical background I realized that the seminars weren't that good, but we got a week off to improve our knowledge followed by a week on the road to teach a three day seminar. The seminars were usually held in large cities. The seminar attendees were asked to fill out evaluations of the seminars. If we got a bad one, we would simply throw it away. We would sometimes be end played by attendees mailing in their evaluations, in which case the evaluations were always negative. I didn't bother to mention to management that the content of the seminars wasn't that great.

Our seminar in New York City was at a Holiday Inn near Times Square. Taking the elevator down to go out for dinner at night, there were often some very provocatively dressed young women riding down. Out of curiosity, I asked at the front desk what that was about. It turns out that they were pros on their way to work. There was a two-block area in a dimly lit section of the city where the professional ladies would congregate. It seemed like a dumb way of pretending it wasn't going on.

One time in Washington D.C. we were at our usual hotel and wondered where all the students were. Sylvania had changed hotels without telling us, so the three of us went racing across town during rush hour to the other side of the beltway. Fortunately, the locally hired receptionist had checked everybody in, and we were only a few minutes late. Another time a commercial airliner crashed into the Potomac River right behind our hotel.

Initially, business was good, but as the economy soured, attendance waned. The handwriting was on the wall. I would come back from a teaching assignment and a whole room full of seminar teachers would be gone along with the furniture.

When I had worked briefly in Santa Barbara, I was asked by a government representative to witness noise figure measurements of a parametric amplifier of the type I used to design. The designer of the amplifier was an engineer-inventor who had formed his own company. We kept in touch, and on a seminar-teaching trip to Los Angeles; he came down to the airport hotel where I was staying and wanted me to invest in his company. He had patented a miles-per-gallon meter for cars and had also designed and patented broadband microwave frequency mixers, which no one else had been able to develop. He charged a fortune for them. I said I would consider investing in his company, if I could work there for a year. Sitting at the hotel bar that night, I got involved in a conversation with two friendly young ladies and presented them with the details of the offer. They advised me that as long as I didn't invest everything I had, go for it. It seemed like good advice. It was also an opportunity to relocate to Santa Barbara, which is a pretty good place to hang out. In hindsight, I think that the young ladies at the bar where professionals.

CHAPTER 12

SANTA BARBARA

HAVING PLAYED DUPLICATE bridge for a number of years, I would play once or twice a week in Santa Barbara. One night as I gazed across the bridge room, I saw this pretty blonde who looked interesting. For some reason she didn't look married. I said to myself, that's the woman I am going to marry, not knowing anything about her. This is from someone who never remotely considered getting married, which included some very attractive women in South America. A few days later the director of the bridge club called and said she had a nice partner for me. Because I was new in town, I had asked the bridge directors to let me know if someone was looking for a game. For some reason I knew who it would be. Nothing unusual happened, when we played bridge that night, but later I got a call from my new bridge partner inviting me over to her house for dinner and bridge with another couple. Of the long time girlfriends that I had, I can only remember twice having a dinner cooked for me. This despite my taking them to numerous expensive dinners in restaurants, but then none of them had previously been married. It was surprising that the other woman invited to play bridge was a very attractive, single, flirtatious blonde. I would have expected Ugly Betty to be the other woman. One thing I liked about Georgia was that she did not drink alcoholic beverages. My last girl friend in Boston drank like a fish, and sometimes we didn't know how we got home. It is hard to be in

a restaurant and have more than one drink sitting across from someone who doesn't drink. After a short courtship, we were married in
Las Vegas and along with Georgia's teenage son, John, from her first
marriage, we moved into a new home in Santa Barbara overlooking
the Channel Islands. John was a great kid and to this day we get along
really well.

Georgia had an interesting background. She had grown up in Los
Angeles. Georgia's parents owned and operated a restaurant in Long
Beach on Alameda Boulevard. When Georgia was four years old
the Long Beach earthquake struck. Georgia was on the toilet when
the restaurant came crashing down. Georgia's mother convinced a
male customer to go back inside and rescue Georgia, which he did.
Another customer was not so lucky, when he went back into the restaurant to get a pack of cigarettes, the whole building came down,
burying him in the rubble. Georgia, her four siblings, and parents
lived in a tent with no plumbing until a replacement restaurant and
upstairs living quarters could be rebuilt.

Georgia's grandmother had been a movie and stage actress,
which prompted Georgia's mother to have Georgia and her older sister take dance lessons. At the tender age of fourteen Georgia and
her older sister were sent out on a ten-month tour with a traveling
dance company that played in such places as Kansas City, St. Louis,
Boston and Montreal. A featured performer was Sally Rand doing her
famous fan dance. Sally was getting a little over- the-hill by then, but
they still came to see her perform. The tour was quite an education.
After going to UCLA for one year, Georgia's grandmother got her into
the movie studios where Georgia worked as a dancer in musicals
and also as a water ballet performer in several Ester Williams movies.
Georgia mentioned that there was always a double for Ester when she
was supposed to be diving from a diving board. Having worked with
Marilyn Monroe, Georgia believed that contrary to the accepted the-
ory, Marilyn would never have committed suicide. Georgia worked
on such movies as An American in Paris, Singing in the Rain, Good
News, and Son of Paleface. Georgia enjoyed being in the choral group

that first sang the song Silver Bells in the movie The Lemon Drop Kid. She was shown in a long white evening gown in the newspaper ads for the movie, I Can Get It for You Wholesale. Georgia lived within walking distance to MGM in Culver City, where she often worked. Other studios were also close by.

Of her many stories of the studios and the stars, one stands out. She was working on location at the Long Beach Airport. Cary Grant, the star of the picture, offers her a ride home. On the way to her house he asked if she wanted to go on a cruise with him and Howard Hughes to Catalina. The answer was no. The next day when she showed up for work, she was told that her services were no longer needed. Georgia was only 18 at the time; Cary Grant was in his 40's. That studio never asked Georgia to work for them again. Also, 20th Century Fox called Georgia and asked her what had she done to Cary Grant? Apparently, he was calling other studios to try to get Georgia black-listed. The story doesn't say much for Cary Grant's character.

Georgia worked in the movies up until the time that she became pregnant with her son for a total of about six years and briefly after John was born. Georgia's first husband became a very successful homebuilder after they were married. They retired to Santa Barbara at an early age.

In the meantime the electronics industry along with the economy in general had gone completely to hell. The majority stockholder of the company that I had invested in had a choice of laying himself off or me. No one was hiring in Santa Barbara. I was able to hire into EG&G in nearby Goleta. Three hundred people had applied for the job. I had to take a technical test before they would even talk to me. For the second test I had to explain an electronic circuit. It was similar to a circuit that I had just been working on so I was able to explain its functionality well. Unfortunately, after nine months the company decided to discontinue the product line and our entire department was laid off. The economy had not improved. Although being unemployed, I paid a man to paint our street number on the curb. He said he was a Ph. D. in chemistry and couldn't find a job. Through a stroke of good luck, I was able to find another job. The bad news was that it was a long commute to Oxnard and it didn't pay very well. I was barely making enough money to pay the bills.

CHAPTER 13

KWAJALIEN REVISITED

OUT OF A clear blue sky RCA calls and offers me my old boss's job at the Kwajalien Missile Test Site. Since they had obviously tracked me down, I quoted them a base salary of 50% more that I was currently making. They didn't even flinch. I should have asked for more. The bonus was now only 25%, but there was 10-12 hours of overtime pay each week. Housing was free, no utility bills, tax-free status, etc. After much discussion with my wife, we decided to take the job. Georgia's son, John, had just graduated from high school and would stay in our home in Santa Barbara.

Having lived on Kwajalien before, it was not much of an adjustment for me but for Georgia, it was a whole new ballgame. On Kwajalien we never met anyone else from California. The married people on our project were either from Boston or New Jersey. One of the many forms of entertainment was free movies. One of the theaters was open air. It was great to sit out in the warm evening air with the stars so bright because of the clear, non-polluted air. We would bring our ponchos, for the occasional passing shower. One of the musicals that Georgia had been in was playing, and our next-door neighbor said that there was a girl in the movie that looked just like Georgia. The neighbor could not comprehend that someone that she knew had been in a movie.

With the very good compensation and very low expenses you

would think that everybody would be fat, dumb, and happy. But when we arrived there was a burning issue, that if you didn't park your bicycle in the bicycle racks at the local department store, you could get a two-dollar fine. They must have rescinded the edict, because there was no revolution. When a family had acquired approximately $50,000 in savings, there was often a notable shift in attitude. It was an "I've got mine so to heck with you," attitude. It was actually entertaining at times.

In addition to free movie theaters there were men's and women's softball leagues, tennis leagues, bowling leagues, duplicate bridge, basketball leagues, a good library, swimming pools, sandy beaches, snorkeling, scuba diving, deep sea fishing, martial arts classes and free taxi service. Everyone rode bicycles. There were a few vehicles that could be checked out for special purposes. Alcohol was very cheap and there were a lot of private parties plus project parties.

The island had a pecking order depending on your company, status within your company, etc. Also, our project had a pecking order depending on which company you worked for, all of which we totally ignored. It seemed to bother some people that we were good bridge players, good tennis players, and that Georgia had been asked to be a model in a local fashion show. Georgia and I were teamed up to play in a doubles tennis league. We were undefeated in league play, which was no bid deal to us. The players were mostly from the northeast and not that good. However, it bothered other team captains, and they were considering playing some of their best men players against us in doubles, which seemed rather childish.

My immediate supervisor was also the RCA softball team manager. He quizzed me at length about my softball playing ability. I thought, wow; maybe this was like basketball on my first tour of the island, where there had been some really good players. I was actually a better softball player than basketball, having logged thousands of hours playing softball while growing up. Our team had some players who looked like they had never played the game. I was used to playing fast pitch softball; this was slow pitch. All I would do is punch the ball into right field or ground it between the first and second base for a single. Some of our players would swing as hard as they could and consistently fly out. One game I made what was probably the best catch of my life. Running away from the infield in the outfield at full speed, I backhanded a line drive that should have been a home run. On returning to the dugout, our site manager explained how I should have caught the ball. The guy that hit the ball however, thought it was a great catch. We did have a few good players and won about half our games.

After working on the same radar system for two years, I was transferred to a newer radar system in another building. The engineer that was in charge of the receiving subsystem had designed most of the equipment, and he was the only one who understood its operation well. I was to be his understudy. Management was concerned that he would leave site in a huff someday as he was somewhat unpredictable.

One change from when I was previously on Kwajalien was that there was more tolerance about people having affairs. It was common knowledge that various married people were engaged in extramarital relationships. It seems that everyone on island was aware of it except the spouses of the involved parties. There were however some strange rules. The Arab oil embargo was going on and the island Army commander decreed that there would be no streetlights on at night. The result was that a teenage girl riding her bicycle at night fell and died as a result. My own wife severely sprained her ankle while walking home one night. We got our normal consignment of oil with not enough storage room resulting in the gravel roads getting extra coatings of oil. When we would go on vacation, Honolulu would be lit up bright as day, so much for the oil savings. Another strange rule was that cats were to be on leashes. There were a number of strays that helped to keep the rat population down. We had adopted one, and she of course roamed free. No one paid any attention to the rule. The Marshallese had their own broadcast TV station on their island, but the residents of Kwajalien were forbidden to watch it. A senior scientist with Lincoln Labs had his TV set, that he had smuggled onto the island, confiscated. It was claimed that the Marshallese broadcast pornographic movies. How would anyone know? Our island for some reason could not have a TV station.

We were able to get off island about every four or five months. In arriving at Honolulu we would head straight for Waikiki and usually stay at the Sheraton Waikiki right on the beach. We liked to see people who we didn't know, eat in good restaurants, and enjoy the beach. We never ran into anyone from Kwajalien.

The employees of the other RCA company were required once a year to go back to their Moorestown facility in New Jersey. We found it puzzling that they would then spend their own money to fly to the Caribbean for vacation. On returning to Kwajalien they would often stay at the Ala Moana Hotel in Honolulu next to the Ala Moana Shopping Center so they could shop, ignoring Waikiki altogether. Well, each to his own.

We often went to the beach early to avoid the crowds. On a nearly deserted beach, if some group came and sat down right next to us or even right in front of us, they were often from New Jersey. The Canadians were usually the friendliest people.

On one vacation we went to Acapulco. We didn't find the hotel staff very nice. Both my wife and I speak enough Spanish to get the gist of what is being said. One night returning to our hotel by taxi, we were stopped at a police checkpoint. One of the cops shines his flashlight on my wife's hands. If she had more expensive looking jewelry on, who knows what might have happened. Midway through our stay we decided that we would much rather be in Hawaii and left early. The people at the Acapulco airport were downright scary. On coming and going through Hawaii we would always stay at Waikiki or go to one of the other islands for a few days. On one visit to Maui my wife and I went to a native Hawaiian show in a very large outdoor theater. On walking by the stage I noticed one of the hula dancers checking me out and turning and saying something to one of the other dancers. I said to my wife that I must be getting volunteered for something. Sure enough, during the show the dancer came over and dragged me up on the stage. Being somewhat mentally prepared, I got a nice ovation for doing my rendition of the Tahitian hula.

While on Kwajalien, the majority stockholder of the company that I worked for in Santa Barbara decided to buy out the other stockholders so I was able to sell my stock at a nice profit. I was never sure that the investment would ever pay off.

After three years on Kwajalien, it was time to leave. There were families that had children born on the island and that graduated from high school there. Our favorite ocean side restaurant was closed down as was the officer's club restaurant, leaving only the enlisted men's mess hall if you wanted to eat out. Throughout our stay there was very little in the way of fresh fruits or vegetables brought in. Our visiting entertainment shows disappeared when contractor Bell Labs left the island. When the federal government would threaten to cut back benefits, Bell Labs would say fine; we're leaving. After their departure, the other contractors didn't have the intestinal fortitude to stand up to the government.

CHAPTER 14

BACK TO THE STATES

SINCE GEORGIA HAD never lived in the East as an adult, we thought it would be fun to take a job with RCA in Florida. Along with our wild cat that we adopted, we moved to Cocoa Beach so I could work at Patrick AFB. We were able to very cheaply rent a two-bedroom house on half an acre with a lighted tennis court right on the beach. The drive to work in the morning on Route A1A was so perilous that I would leave home early and spend the time reading the newspaper before the work day began. Driving home was fun, however, as there were often young ladies returning from the beaches crossing A1A in their bikinis and carrying their surfboards. Being the gentleman that I was, I would often stop and allow them to cross the road.

The local Floridians at work would bad mouth California about earthquakes until I pointed out that more people were killed on A1A in a month than had been killed in earthquakes in California during the past ten years. Driving home one night in the dark after eating out with my wife, we came upon four or five guys sitting and standing in the middle of A1A.

While playing tennis one night after work, a tourist was killed by lightening a hundred yards from where we were playing with our metal rackets. Florida is acknowledged as the lightening capital of the world. In the local newspaper there would be stories about tourists going out swimming in the ocean and not returning, like it was some kind of mystery. No point in alarming the tourists about sharks.

If the weather report said there was a 20% chance of rain, you could take it to the bank. Sometimes it rained so hard that you could not see to drive, and you had to pull off the road. Every heavy rain there would be reports of someone driving off a causeway and drowning. They were not big on breakdown lanes or guardrails.

At some point I would be required to go to Ascension Island in the Atlantic for several months without my wife to install the radar system that we were assembling. This did not seem like a lot of fun. So when an RCA recruiter was calling to recruit engineers for work in New Jersey and later at NSA headquarters in Maryland, I signed up. Unfortunately, I didn't have a good technical background for the job, but things worked out well enough.

Working in Camden, New Jersey was very different. There were these things called expressways that had no controlled access. On my first day driving to work I saw three rear end collisions. After that, I drove to work on the surface streets of Camden. Although Camden had a very high crime rate, I never had any problems. I did notice however that the police patrolled in pairs and the officers were very large. Actually, I had a choice of taking a bus, the high-speed rail line, or driving to work. RCA had a parking lot with high fences topped with concertina wire, armed guards with dogs, and cameras. There were still reports of muggings. One morning a man was robbed walking from the parking lot into his building. In the executive parking lot thieves were arrested as they were going along removing batteries from the cars. Across the street from my building was a parking lot with no fence with an old man in a rocking chair minding the store. For fifty cents you could park there all day. It was worth a try. The parking lot must have been owned by the mob or the muggers, since I never heard of any problems there. The only two buildings on our block were a bank and the RCA building that I worked in. One noon hour shortly before Christmas four bank robbers emerged from the bank just as the police arrived. There was a massive gun battle, which the robbers lost, 4-0. The last work day before Christmas the party at work started well before noon with booze flowing freely. As far as I know, everyone kept their clothes on, but that was about all you could say. Since I left rather early, who knows what happened.

While working at Camden, the RCA management on Kwajalien requested that I temporarily come back because my former boss left in a huff and no one was knowledgeable of the radar receiving system on the last radar that I worked on. Fortunately, my current boss said no. It was at least nice to be needed.

One day I was taking the high-speed rail line home. After I descended to the station, there were these four young black men around a bench, who were obviously high on something. I figured that if things got dicey, I could sprint up the stairs. Down the stairs comes a nice looking young black girl. After she sizes up the situation, she comes and stands on the other side of me as close as she can. The guys are now screaming and making strange noises. We were both hoping that the train would come real soon. As soon as the car doors opened, we both leaped in.

While living in New Jersey my younger brother, Brian, graduated from South Dakota State and true to form, there were no job offers. My boss at RCA hired him to work as a programmer including per diem so he was able to save some money.

After 18 months of soaking up per diem in New Jersey, Georgia and I thought it would be nice to live in the Washington D.C. area for a while so I asked to be transferred to NSA at Ft. Meade Maryland. New Jersey had been fun. We were right across the Delaware River from Philadelphia and were able to go in for plays, the symphony orchestra, baseball and football games, and dinner.

We bought a townhouse in Crofton, Maryland, which was close to Ft. Meade. Our project required a top-secret, special intelligence clearance, which required a polygraph test. During my polygraph test I nearly fell asleep, probably due to my yoga training, which helps you to relax. It was interesting that 50% of the retired military, who had top secret clearances in the service, failed the polygraph test. Alcohol had a lot to do with the rejections. Some project personnel couldn't prove where they were born because of poor record keeping. While at NSA, on occasion, permanent employees would divulge highly classified information to me, some things that are probably still classified today. It was not information that I had a need to know.

While living in Crofton we would take the subway in to D.C. and visit the museums, and tour the White House and monuments. Georgia became the tour guide for visiting relatives.

While working at Ft. Meade I would sometimes ride share with another engineer. It was a winding drive through the woods and not very interesting. One day I happened to mention a stock investment that didn't work out well. He seemed overjoyed at that news. So to pass the time I would make up outlandish tales of stock losses, which he would really relish. People would come up to me at work and gleefully bring up these tales of horrendous losses. No one seemed to catch on. I did not count these people among my friends, but it did provide some entertainment.

Coming out of work one afternoon there were about five inches of snow on the ground. The usual twenty-minute commute home took one and a half hours. Maryland must have had snowplows; it's just that I never saw one. After that, at the first falling snowflake I was on my way home. If it snowed overnight, I would wait until the rush hour was over before going in to work. It was clear that some of the drivers had never driven on snow before, scary. The state did not waste money on breakdown lanes or lane dividers that were visible at night when it was raining.

After about 10 months at NSA, I realized that the job I had was not going to last much longer. We had a beautiful fall day with low humidity, which was unusual in Maryland. Bingo! Most days in Southern California were like that. It was time to move on. I was at a job interview in Westlake Village, California. It soon dawned on me that the recruiter has marketed me as a software engineer, which I was not. Well, I might as well fake it.

Fate intervenes once again. While I am in the plant, the System Engineering group calls my home in Maryland and asks about my availability. Georgia said as a matter of fact, he is in your facility right now. Bunker-Ramo moved us back to California. In the mean time, we had bought a home in Citrus Heights near Sacramento where John, Georgia's son and wife, Kathy, were living, site unseen. The longer you stay away from California, the more difficult it is to buy back into the housing market.

After a year at Bunker-Ramo, it was clear that our project had a limited future. Fortunately, Litton Data Command, just down the street, was hiring for a huge job in Saudi Arabia. This was the kind of project that you dream about. We had good raises, twice a year. The Christmas parties were great. Several 22-carat gold chains would be given out and there was free wine at each table. For the first few years the bands played 1940's music, so Georgia and I would crash the party next door, which was usually the "City of Hope" party, which always had a name band playing. We had engineering socials often with free booze.

Litton was staffing up. It is not easy to decide if someone would make a good employee or not, based on a fifteen-minute interview. A good rule of thumb was that if the applicant exhibited any form of unusual behavior to exclude them from consideration. I would, if possible, arrange to take the applicant to lunch if there was any interest on my part, giving me more time to evaluate them. One engineer being interviewed would let out a very loud yawn every few minutes during the interview. Fellow workers would sometimes recommend a friend of theirs, knowing that the candidate was not competent. There was a young, black, West Point graduate looking for a job. I tried to explain to my fellow managers that it was very unusual for such a person to leave the Army, but the person he would be working for was a retired Navy chief, and I think that he liked the idea of having a West Point graduate working for him. The Army man had a real problem showing up for work, and it turns out he had a cocaine habit. When he was fired, he owed the company a fairly large sum of money.

In the meantime my brother Brian had been laid off from RCA and wound up back home in South Dakota. As was the case before, getting a job from South Dakota was not very promising. We invited him out to Westlake Village and on his first interview he got a job at the local IBM facility.

Almost every news story that I have had some knowledge of has been inaccurate. A classic example is the following:

Late one Friday afternoon I walked into the office of an engineer that I supervised. He said that there was some kind of electronic device connected to his telephone line. I took the cover plate off of the phone line and sure enough, there was a circuit card connected to the phone line. It looked like something a home hobbyist would build, not something a spy would install. I called plant security and informed them of the situation. Security sent over two electricians to look at it. Our facility was full of communications engineers, who could probably analyze the situation very well.

The next morning on the radio I heard a news story that said a listening device was found in a computer room at our facility and that plant security had recently been breached. First of all we didn't have a "computer room" at our facility, and I can't imagine who had figured out that it was a listening device. The story was repeated on the local Los Angeles TV evening news that night by none other than Connie Chung. It also made headlines in the Riyadh, Saudi Arabia, English language newspaper.

The actual story was that the FBI concluded that it was a device that could be used by someone to call into the facility and use the company WATTS lines to make long distance calls. It was probably installed by an engineer, who had worked in that office, and who left the company after a short time. We had very little classified work on our project and none in the office area where the device was found. The breaching of plant security turned out to be that a low level employee on a Sunday had climbed over the fence between our two buildings and let in his girl friend so he could show her around. When he let her in an emergency exit door, an alarm went on at the guard station and a guard on duty went over and threw them out. There was no retraction or follow up news story in the news media.

There was a large contingent of young Saudi soldiers in training at Litton. There had been an acrimonious battle in the local newspaper to keep them from being housed in the area. They were hardly battle-tested veterans. When the swing shift would come to work, they would be marched around a parking lot to sober them up; so much for adhering to their Moslem tenants. My office overlooked the parking lot where the soldiers parked. If you valued your car, it was not wise to park in that lot. The Saudis were not great drivers.

Employees were offered a 25% bonus to go to Saudi Arabia. No thank you. People who went there and came back to California after two or three years actually lost money, if they had sold their homes. A very lucrative policy was put in place for people who went to Saudi temporarily. Normally, personnel were rotated out every seven weeks. If you would stay for 14 or 21 weeks, the company would pay you the equivalent of the airfares. We flew first class. A 25% bonus and a hefty per diem were also included.

CHAPTER 15

SAUDI ARABIA

AS PART OF the program, a Litton installed, countrywide, troposcatter communications system was being tested in Saudi. The first link test ended in disaster. The test failed and the Litton test director, apparently in a fit of anger, pushed the Norwegian test witness, who was hired by the Saudis, out of a communications shelter. This was not a good start. I was asked to take over the test director position.

The first thing that I did was to have our management ask the Saudis to change the upper baseband frequency slot of the voice frequency channels where noise was being measured to a slightly lower frequency. It was seemingly a harmless change, but probably fundamental to the success of the test effort.

For amusement I had been taking Arabic language lessons from a fellow Litton employee back in California, who had taught at West Point. I worked hard at learning the language and would chat with the Saudi military personnel who were at Litton for training. It turned out that the military officers in Saudi didn't want to speak Arabic to Americans. One of our program mangers was Lebanese and spoke fluent Arabic, but he didn't have any better luck. On meeting the occasional Bedouin in the desert I was able to use the language. At our remote troposcatter sites I would pick up on the Arabic conversations of the military personnel and comment. They decided that I was a CIA spy, why not?

In Riyadh there was the Ba'atha Souk where you could buy quality cloth and have dress pants, jackets, and suits tailor made at very reasonable prices. It was hard to get anyone to go with me to the souk at night. The parking garage was pitch black with no one around; and when you strolled around the souk, you rarely saw any Americans or Europeans. As you passed by the various stalls you could hear comments in Arabic about "Englizees," aka Caucasians. However, I never had any trouble.

One of the funniest things that happened was that the Saudi soldiers that had been to Litton for training would sing along with the Christian hymns that the BBC would broadcast on the HF radio on Sunday morning, which was a regular work day in Saudi Arabia.

One day I witnessed a three-car accident in the parking lot as the soldiers were leaving the site; it had to be seen to be believed.

I pointed out to the Norwegian test witnesses that I was half Norwegian, that I was a Lutheran, and that my mother took confirmation in the Lutheran church in Norwegian. I also bought a Norwegian phrase book and would greet the Norwegians with a few words in their language.

Every 90 days I would have to get my tourist visa renewed outside the country. Litton, bless their hearts, would let me select where, and they would fly my wife there on business class. We usually chose London. I was lucky that renewal fell around Ramadan a couple of times, which delayed visa renewal. It was tough duty hanging out in London or Stockholm for 10-12 days on company expense. We were also allowed to stay at any hotel we wanted to. While in London I would always stay at the Inn-on-the-Park, a five star hotel. When checking in you would sit at a desk. I didn't need to identify who I was, they knew. At the breakfast buffet I asked to sign the chit. The response was, "Oh no Mr. Linder, there is no need to sign anything." Again, they knew who I was; don't ask me how. To test the hotel's flexibility I arrived at 6:30 AM after a flight from Saudi without telling them about my early arrival. They were very apologetic and said that when the breakfast room opened at 7:00 AM to have breakfast on them; then my room would be ready. I strolled through the park down to Buckingham Palace to kill time until 7:00. One unusual aspect of the hotel was that in the evening at the restaurant there would be older men dining with very attractive, much younger, well-dressed women. I was about 95% sure that the women were pros or maybe mistresses. My vote was that they were high-end call girls.

On one visit to London my wife and I were having afternoon tea at the Inn-on-the–Park Hotel. There was a rather strict dress code. In walks Pia Isadora, her billionaire husband, Meshulam Riklis, and two other men, all in sweat clothes. They sat in the booth next to us; nothing was said to them about any dress code.

After working and traveling in many foreign countries it was interesting to note that sex is treated as a commodity in most places. Obtaining sex, even in Moslem Pakistan, was not difficult. I don't know if the two are really tied together, but overseas if a woman shows interest in a man, she usually has something specific on her mind. In the US women often come on to a man with absolutely no intent of carrying it any further. Overseas the relationship between men and women seems to be more honest. If sex can easily be purchased, then relationships would tend to be based on more than just sex. If a man believes sex to be a commodity, it seems to actually improve faithfulness to his spouse.

During the long term, tropo link testing, Litton was often their worst enemy. One day arriving at our Riyadh North tropo site, I saw a Litton employee carrying voltmeters out to a vehicle in the parking lot. They looked like the voltmeters from our test configuration, which we used to monitor tropo link noise levels. When I asked him what he was doing, he said the meters were due calibration. He had walked into the control building and removed the meters from our online test configuration without asking or telling anyone. I told him that if ever came on site again for any reason, he would die a very slow and painful death. Part of the deal for me to run the testing was that I was to have total and complete control of the test effort. I didn't want some desk jockey second-guessing every decision that I made. The customer could have made us restart the testing, but after I begged forgiveness, we were allowed to continue testing. Another blunder was when I arrived at site one morning, I was reading the log from the night shift and noticed that soon after the night shift came on duty, the diesel backup generator for the control building came on. The generator had an eight- hour fuel tank, and as I looked up at the clock, the power went off. There was a standing order that if anything unusual happened, I was to be called immediately, day or night. We had three diesel mechanics living at our Litton compound, that could have come out to site and trouble shot the problem. One of the night shift technicians said he didn't like the way I was talking to him about the incident. My response was that I was going try to get him fired.

There was an engineer TDY at our site and when he had finished his assignment, I thanked him for a job well done. He said that in 20 years at Litton no one had ever thanked him for anything, sad but probably true.

One last hiccup happened after we ran a five-site, voice com-munications test, which required every equipment shelter to be able to talk to every other shelter. It was a lengthy and time-consuming effort. The site technicians agreed to come in on their own time on Saturday and run the test, which was somewhat of a miracle, since their contracts said that they were to work a forty-hour week. At a test review meeting the Litton Quality Control monitor kept insisting that the test did not "flow" well. I pointed out that no style points were awarded, unlike synchronized swimming. These morons in the meeting, including two directors, wanted to rerun the test. We had a program manager who was a holy terror, and many people were deathly afraid of him for good reason. Out of desperation I said, that I had discussed the test results with the program manger and that he agreed that the test had passed. Surprisingly, no one questioned the validity of the statement and didn't have the intestinal fortitude to ask him. I would use the same ploy again, whenever it was needed. No one ever caught on.

While testing at a remote tropo site, which was out in the desert, I would take walks. One day on returning to the control building, lying on the stairs, was a sand viper, which is a very poisonous snake and exactly the color of the desert sand, so much for walks in the desert. There was a nasty looking thing, which was called a camel spider and looked like a crab. One day a camel spider was chasing an engineer across the parking lot; he was not one of our more macho guys.

Of the several tropo sites that I visited, one was very interesting. It was on a very high, steep hill. There was just enough room for the very large antennas and associated buildings and living quarters at the top. After breakfast, I would sit outside and have my coffee next to a sheer drop off of about 1500 feet. The view was impressive.

After 18 months in Saudi Arabia, it was time to go home. The testing effort was going well and was about 80% complete. I did not want my wife to come to Saudi Arabia, because of the severe restrictions that women have to put up with. After she had gone to the gold souk and loaded up on 22-carat gold jewelry, she would want to go home and would try to get me to leave. It is not a fun place for most westerners. Compensation turned out to be about double salary mostly free of federal taxes, which you hate to give up. But 18 months in Saudi Arabia was enough. On leaving Saudi the company threw a large going away dinner for me at one of the quality hotels in Riyadh, which was really a nice gesture.

There are some real misconceptions about life in Saudi Arabia. Many foreigners made their own wine, which was often quite good. At the grocery stores there would be pallets of sugar right next to cases of grape juice. You only had to smuggle yeast into the country to make wine. The American women would put their laciest lingerie on top of their clothes in their suitcases and when the Muslim customs agents would open up their suitcases, they would quickly close them again, not finding the yeast. You could readily buy bootleg booze, named siddiqui (my friend in Arabic), which was powerful stuff. At a compound for mostly Europeans next to the Litton compound in Riyadh the women sunbathed topless at the swimming pool. It was just my luck to arrive shortly after some Saudi having lunch at the compound complained and the custom was ended.

There was a tropo site near Dhahran, which was near the Persian Gulf. To get there you had to drive a narrow road that went through a small mud brick Saudi village. Often standing by the side of the road would be a nice looking woman dressed in a beautiful silk gown with a very minimal scarf covering her head. I had no idea what that was about and thought it best not to find out. While going to the site one day I gave three Egyptian engineers, hired by our subcontractor, a ride. When we got to the guard station out came several Saudi soldiers with their rifles pointed at the car and demanded to see their site passes. This had never happened before, so much for trusting their fellow Arab Muslim brothers.

There are a lot of foreign nurses working in Saudi, most of who are looking for boyfriends and or husbands. A young engineer for Litton that I had recruited was working late one night. My cohorts and I decided that he needed something else to do with his time. One of the guys had a girlfriend, who supervised the women's dorm at one of the large hospitals. We got her to meet Joe, size him up, and then find a suitable girlfriend for him. Joe is tall and laid back. She found a nice, tall Dutch girl. They were a perfect match and eventually got married.

Some of the Litton personnel took wild chances. Two employees sat with their girlfriends in front of a mosque one night drinking alcohol. There was a "Christian bypass" on the freeway around Mecca but our personnel knew a back road into Mecca and would go there which was of course a no-no for infidels. At one site the technicians tried to smuggle a western female doctor in a large box into their compound and were caught. An engineer stopped to aid a motorist and the driver turned out to be a young, attractive Saudi woman. Women were forbidden to drive in Saudi. She would show up at our compound to see him. While sitting at a traffic light I would sometimes glance over at other drivers and see some very slender hands on the steering wheel. With the headscarves and robes you really didn't know who was driving a car.

One of our troposcatter site managers was returning to Saudi and was going through Customs. He remembered that he had a marijuana cigarette in his pocket and he quickly swallowed it, but someone in Customs saw him swallow something. He was thrown in jail and eventually turned loose and sent home. He had some wild tales to tell about the kind of people that he was with in jail. One man had a tiny airline bottle of alcohol that he put in a soda on a flight to Saudi. On Saudia Airlines alcohol is forbidden. Someone reported him and he was thrown in jail for who knows how long. On the other hand, a Saudi sitting next to me on a Pan Am flight coming in country proceeded to get drunk out of his mind. One of the many joys about leaving Saudi on a foreign carrier was to have a drink after reaching cruising altitude. When the Saudi women were leaving the country, they changed out of their abayas into expensive western clothing, as soon as the "fasten your seat belt lights" went out.

On one of my trips back to the States I went through the Far East. Staying overnight in Bangkok, I went to the hotel coffee shop to get a good milk shake and hamburger, two things that were hard to find in Saudi. The coffee shop was staffed by young women in beautiful, long, silk evening gowns. They were in pairs where one girl was the trainee. That was quite a change from Saudi where the staff and patrons were all male, except for the family dining section. Malaysian Airlines advertised how great their first class service was. I was waiting for my flight in Hong Kong in the departure lounge when a representative walked up to me and said, "Mister Linder would you like to board your flight now?" How he knew who I was and was flying first class on Malaysian Airlines, I have no idea. By contrast, I was on a Pan Am flight and when going to board, there was a long line. I went to the head of the line and asked if they had first class boarding. After some grumbling, they reluctantly let me board ahead of tourist class.

Driving in Saudi is probably as dangerous as any place in the world. On our project just about every driver that did not drive very defensively was involved in some type of an accident. At traffic lights I would try to stop next to the big steel poles, which supported the traffic signals, hoping that someone roaring up to the light would not want to hit a steel pole. Hitting other cars didn't seem to bother some of the other drivers. The Saudis did not take away crashed vehicles; they were just pushed to the side of the road. The few times in rained in Riyadh, the collection would grow. Towards the end of my stay, they did start a cleanup. I was assigned a Chevy Suburban, which is a good-sized vehicle. On the numerous traffic circles you could bluff out most drivers, but you had to watch out for what I thought must be the really devout Muslims, who knew Allah would protect them. They were totally unfazed to see a Suburban bearing down on them. The traffic circles themselves were unusual in that there were very large and had unusual sculptures in the middle of the circle, in one case a giant bicycle. There were drivers there from all over the world. The Europeans tended to drive fast and were somewhat reckless. If someone did something to purposely annoy other drivers, I would try to determine their nationality. Usually, they looked American.

I returned to Saudi for a six-month stay in Jeddah to soak up some more bonus money. Jeddah has the hottest, most humid weather that I have ever seen. There were numerous, good tennis players living at the large Litton compound, and we had a large tennis league. No one every played in the daytime. After playing at night, everything you were wearing would be soaked with perspiration.

Jeddah is almost like a different country compared with Riyadh. Saudi women would flirt openly with western men. One night, I and another engineer were out for a drive along a stretch of road that paralleled the Red Sea, which had amusement parks and small stands selling snacks. We stopped at an ice cream stand; there aren't a lot of exciting things to do in Saudi. Sitting on a bench were three young women, with abayas on, who I presumed were Saudi. They spoke very good English and obviously wanted to chat. My friend, who was young and single, was terrified by the idea of talking to Saudi women and insisted we leave, no guts.

During my stay, there was a countrywide test of the entire Litton-built air defense and communications system. The Saudis were allowed to set the test criteria. The test passed, but the Saudis reneged on the deal. The rumor going around was that the Saudis never paid the last 10% owed on any contract.

The Saudia Airline flights for London left at reasonable hours; the foreign carriers left in the middle of the night. It was worth the wait, as being on a Saudia flight was too much like being in the country. On my way home from Saudi I was asked to take numerous small parcels and letters back to the States. At Heathrow Airport in London I left one suitcase in Left Luggage overnight. The next morning checking in with Pan Am, the ground crew seemed unusually nervous. I asked to watch the x-ray of my own luggage, as I didn't want to have someone slip something into my Left Luggage suitcase. It turns out that it was the last flight, prior to the Lockerbee flight. I have to believe that somebody knew something. There was also a rumor that US embassy and consulate people in Germany were instructed not to fly Pan Am at that time.

After having worked in five different countries, spending time in more overseas places, and working in several locations in the States for different companies, you learn to deal with an endless number of unusual situations. The bottom line is that nothing fazes you. When driving the freeways in the US, it seems that given an unusual situation motorists tend to freeze up. One good example is that after clearing an accident on the freeway, some motorists continue to drive 40 mph for some time, although the road ahead of them is completely free of traffic.

CHAPTER 16

BACK HOME

ON RETURNING TO Litton in Agoura Hills our program was now winding down. Throughout my engineering career there were always lay offs. One of the many reasons for working away from the home office was that you were almost immune to lay offs. One large lay off was to be very "sensitive" to the poor devils getting laid off. It turns out that the morning of the lay off, people from the maintenance department piled cardboard boxes by the door of everyone's office that was being laid off. So much for a sensitive lay off.

I was fortunate to get a position at the Litton DSD division in Van Nuys. The bad news was that I had to take a 20% pay cut as the good salaries on the lucrative Saudi contract were out of line with salaries at DSD. There were no other jobs available. The project was to manufacture, build and test shelterized air traffic control equipment for the US Air Force and Marine Corps.

On my second day on the job I was told, "Oh, these 45 engineers work for you." No extra pay or promotion, of course. The next few weeks were challenging. It worked out well for my boss; he supervised four people including myself. His favorite trick was to raise hell about something every week, usually late Friday afternoon. One time it was about some scratches on a wooden workbench, which may have been there five days or five years. He was on a very short leash with his own boss. He used to do some very strange things like hypnotizing female employees in his office at lunchtime behind closed doors. To get rid of him I brought up a subject, that I knew would set him off with reliable witnesses on hand. Sure enough, he exploded. I went to his boss with the story and my troublesome boss was removed. Later, my removed boss was in a staff meeting and after 20 minutes into the meeting, he casually mentioned that one of the engineers had turned on a communications shelter and forgot to turn on the cooling fans, saying somehow it must be my fault. Horrified, I went racing out to the shelter to turn the fans on. It takes all kinds.

One of our tasks was to perform a long-term reliability test on two shelters that went on 24 hours a day, seven days a week. The engineer responsible for the testing wanted to go on a field assignment in Florida. I volunteered to do the testing so that I could better understand the functions of the system. This was in addition to supervising 45 people. The test was completed successfully and there was a large meeting with the customer and various Litton departments to assess the test results. Call it intuition. I was suspicious of one of the customer's test witnesses, a retired Marine non-com. In the meeting he said that I had cheated on the testing, and that the test should be rerun. Fortunately, I had evidence to refute his accusation and had mentally rehearsed my response. His sole purpose, I think, was to cause trouble.

About the same time there was some reorganization going on. I was told that a certain secretary was going to be transferred to our department. I thought we were friends, and one day I causally mentioned that I heard that she "might" be coming to our department. Next day I was called into the office of the boss of my supervisor. There were my boss, his boss, and a Human Resources representative present. The story was that I had somehow threatened the secretary. This outrageous nonsense was perpetuated by a Director, that I often played bridge with during the lunch hour in his office. He was someone that I also thought was a friend. I pointed out that about once a week someone would come up to me and tell me that I was being transferred, going to some field assignment, etc. The question was,

"Should I run to HR every time someone came up with some dopey rumor?" HR dropped the investigation.

The moral to the above stories is that there is a certain segment of the population that delights in causing trouble. This same Director tried to do me in on a couple of other occasions for no reason. He later died of a heart attack at a young age in the office next to where I was attending a meeting. The company made grief consolers available. I doubt that anyone made use of one.

Our project had a large budget and when some department wanted to get rid of an engineer, rather than lay them off, they would wind up on our doorstep. We took in some really unusual personnel. One thing I did learn was that good ideas can come from just about anyone, not just the star performers.

The Litton facility in Van Nuys was closed and sold so we moved back to Agoura Hills, which was much closer to home and was a much nicer facility. My next assignment was to head up a group to build control shelters for an anti-missile defense system, and write the self-off test procedures, and also to maintain a software test lab. Our prime contractor, Lockheed, did not get along well with our software development group. One meeting nearly came to blows. When the main antagonist from Lockheed came to our facility to witness shelter hardware sell-off, I went out of my way to be accommodating. It turns out that he wrote a letter to Litton complimenting my group on their effort. Quite by accident, I heard about the letter and with the help of the Program Manager's secretary I found the letter in the piles of papers on his desk. I inserted the letter into the personnel files of the test engineers who did the sell-off.

There was a large meeting with Litton and the customer. I had to talk to my boss about something important and as quietly and unobtrusively as possible, I slipped into the meeting to ask him a question. It dawned on me that the local Lockheed representative was in the process of praising my efforts on the project. If I had not stumbled into the meeting, I would never have known. One of my favorite sayings was that your reward for doing a good job was that you would probably not be laid off.

Litton got a contract to upgrade the Air Force air defense centers in the US and Canada. Our software director wanted to sell the project a very large, ancient piece of hardware, that took up space in our software development lab, as a radar return simulator. I heard that the Air Force civilian radar expert from Hill AFB in Utah, no name, had a software simulator and would be at a meeting in Ottawa, Canada that I was also attending. Looking around the meeting room, there were about 20 other civilians. I decided one looked like a radar expert, so at lunchtime I asked him if he was from Hill AFB. The bottom line was that he sent me a copy of a software simulator for free, saving the program a nice junk of change. He also sent me a copy of the radar video of an airliner that crashed shortly after take off from JFK in New York. The conspiracy theorists claimed, that it was shot down by a missile. There was no missile visible on the radar video tape.

We were having a large meeting at Litton with the customer. On a break from the meeting a US civil servant asked me an excellent question. I said to bring it up in the meeting. He was a polite, mild mannered type of person. When he introduced the question, the Litton person conducting the meeting, who was also my supervisor, for some unexplainable reason flipped him off. This would be later known as the $2000 flip-off.

Part of my job was to purchase all of the computer hardware and software. I called a large meeting and said okay, tell me what we need to buy. I then published a list of the workstation configurations and other hardware assets, so everyone would know exactly what we were getting. For the software purchases I had the chief software guru give a presentation to the program manager and the director of software on what was needed. The presentation could have been in Russian for all the interest that was shown. During the presentation the presenter was talking about a "sneaker" network. Not being a software person, I asked what a sneaker net was. He said you had to put the info on a CD and physically carry the information to another computer network. It had gone right over the heads of the two directors who were supposed to be screening the software purchases. Did I mention that the program was ill fated?

I assumed that it was my job to set up the computer lab and maintain it. I didn't realize until much later that the computer manufacturer usually had a maintenance contract to do this.

The workstation vendor would put a special connector on their computers so that only monitors sold by them at a much higher price could be used. This was easily bypassed by using a two-dollar adapter so anyone's monitor could be used. Also, they sold computer memory at a high price. It turns out that any manufacturer's memory would work despite dire warnings to the contrary. There were some very experienced people at Litton who believed this nonsense and bought their memory and monitors at the higher prices. Because of the way the contract was written, bonuses were possible for people working on the contract. I used the above cost savings to justify bonuses for Litton employees. My bonus was $2000 so I presumed my boss, who had flipped-off the civil servant, would get at least that much. He got nothing, hence the $2000 flip-off.

Through the years at Litton I was assigned tasks that didn't fit anyone's area of expertise. On the current program there were numerous computer network problems. I was asked to look into the problems and come up with fixes. Knowing next to nothing about computer networks, I was offered help on the task, which I declined. Thirty-five or so problems were identified and solutions implemented or proposed. It would have been nice to at least have gotten an attaboy.

The contract was cancelled by the Air Force because Litton could not come up with a final cost. With the cancellation of the contract and the general downturn in military orders, Litton was going through massive layoffs. Our division went from five buildings to one and a half. On the US-Canadian project, we had bought millions of dollars worth of hardware and software which had to be accounted for and divided up between the US and Canadian Air Forces. A Canadian AF Major was assigned to officially accept everything. He, of course, could make the task easy or impossibly difficult. My boss of flip-off fame went out of his way to make life miserable for the Major, not wise. My boss was laid off shortly thereafter. I went out of my way to humor the Major. The Major agreed to accept items to be shipped to Canada, thus bypassing Canadian Customs, which was a real life-saver. No telling how long the equipment might be under inspection and what import duties might be leveled. Going through Customs is always a tricky business. However, I didn't want to proceed too quickly as there was no work on the horizon at Litton. I was able to drag the effort out for a whole year.

In the meantime, work had started on a job for the Egyptian government, which I was able to work on. One Friday afternoon I got a call from the program manger asking me to take one million dollars out of the hardware budget and send him the new numbers within two hours. Fortunately, I was used to such madness and was able to comply.

To help justify my existence, I acted as the security monitor for a classified lab. The first thing I did was to remove about 70% of the people on the access list. Secretaries, people with no earthly reason for being in a classified area, you name it, were taken off the list. When someone leaves the company, all combination locks that they had access to need to have their combinations changed. This was not done. Engineers would go to lunch and leave classified computer screens up. There were classified, locked file cabinets that no one knew what was inside. The same thing with classified tapes. I have to wonder what our security department did to justify their existence.

One day two armed robbers invaded the credit union at our Moorpark facility at lunchtime. An engineer that I had worked with was inside conducting some transaction. One of the robbers put a gun to his head and said, "Give me your wallet." He said, "No." The robber, instead of blowing his head off, simply reached in his pocket and removed the wallet. The engineer never did come up with an explanation for his mystifying behavior.

Prior to the start of the massive lay offs, Litton had a thriving Toastmasters Club. I joined to enhance my public speaking skills. I noticed that I almost always got a cold on a Monday. It dawned on me that drinking more coffee on the weekend was the culprit. It seemed like a good subject for a speech. After researching the subject of caffeine, it was appalling to read about the very unhealthy effects that it has on the human body. As time wore on, all the Litton members except myself were laid off. So I presided over a club with one Litton member with all the rest coming from outside Litton. Litton paid the dues of all the members, but I neglected to mention the membership makeup.

In the meantime, Northrop-Grumman (N-G) had purchased Litton and was moving our division to another Litton division located in Woodland Hills, California, which was not that far from our Agoura Hills facility. A N-G senior manager came to our facility and gave a talk to our Egyptian project personnel. He said that when a program was in trouble, it was almost always the fault of senior management, not the workers. In my career, my problems were always my problems and company level problems were also the workers' problems. It was refreshing to hear a different story. Looking around the room, I realized that the current senior managers would probably soon become history. They were all removed during the next few weeks.

Later that day I was called to the program manger's office to provide hardware cost information. In walks the N-G chief. The program manager and the chief engineer don't bother to introduce me, so the chief introduces himself and asked what was I presenting and what my position was. He definitely relaxed the atmosphere. Litton management could certainly learn from this guy. For some time I had been trying to convince my project management that a Litton subsidiary company was not honest based on what they were telling us about their products. The N-G chief confirmed this belief in spades based on his direct dealing with them.

Since I had turned 62, I was eager to retire but was hoping Northrop-Grumman would offer some sort of retirement incentive as they were laying off people right and left. Fortunately, an E-mail came out of Human Resources that said if you didn't want to relocate to

Woodland Hills, you could take a layoff. For me that meant 22 weeks of severance pay. The company decided not to honor their policy in my case. After much wrangling and threats of legal action, I was allowed to take a layoff. It was ironic that people who desperately wanted to stay were terminated, but I had to threaten legal action to be cut loose.

After working for 40 years some valuable lessons were learned which you would think would be obvious, but for some strange reason are not. One is to never put anything in writing, including E-mails, that you don't want the whole world to see. This also applies to phone conversations. Never make any kind of negative racial or ethnic comments. Never threaten anyone. In two instances, I felt obligated to report threats that were made to me. In ended very badly for those doing the threatening.

In working for a living, probably the best asset you can have is the ability to get along with and work with people. I started out with a newspaper route at age nine and had a lot of different jobs, giving me the opportunity of interfacing with a lot of people in a lot of different situations. Working with the public is a good place to learn. It seems that some people think that they can behave like an ass, simply because either they can get away with it or they don't know any better. Sooner or later that doesn't work. This would seem like a very good lesson to teach in school at an early age.

The bad judgment of upper management was appalling at times. My boss wanted everyone to work Easter Sunday, for no pay of course. I convinced him that this was not wise. Our big boss was whining that he had to pay a black, single mother engineer for an hour to go and vote. We stood firm and insisted that this was legally required. Our project told the US government that all components that we were purchasing for an overseas program were made in the US. This included computers, monitors, etc. I thought everyone over the age of ten knew that was not true. A brochure had been prepared for the Egyptian government that contained restricted information on

Litton products, which required an export license. No such license had been obtained. I suggested to my management that they opt for a US jail instead of an Egyptian one.

CHAPTER 17

GO FIGURE

AFTER RETIREMENT, I immediately began playing more tennis, doing more yoga, and spending more time at the health club. I began to experience strange physical symptoms. My HMO, that I have a lot of respect for, couldn't figure it out. I told them that I was getting a ton of exercise. Finally, I asked to see a neurologist. A young Indian neurologist, whose mother happened to be a yoga instructor, suggested that I might be dehydrated. This was after endless testing. Bingo! It was like a light going on over my head. After about ten minutes on the Internet, I found my symptoms, one of which was muscle spasms. You would think in southern California that dehydration would be common and easy to diagnose.

CHAPTER 18

THE FOUNTAIN OF YOUTH

MANY PEOPLE ARE looking for a magic pill or even exercise that will make them healthy and happy. The following details the closest thing that I have found to a magic exercise.

Shortly after retirement, I started taking a tai chi class at the local seniors center. One day the instructor had us do a warm pose where we had our hands positioned as if we were holding a beach ball against our chests with our hands cupped around the ball, knees slightly bent, and standing with a straight back. Instinctively, I knew this was a beneficial pose. After class I asked the instructor how long we should stand in the pose. He was a man of very few words and could not offer any suggestions. Several weeks later I was in a bookstore and found a small book with a cover of a couple standing in what looked like static tai chi poses. There on page 24 was a man standing in the pose that I was interested in. The same day that I bought the book, I started doing the poses with the emphasis on the "beach ball" pose. The book is "The Way of Energy," by Master Lam Kam Chuen.

I started with just three minutes of "standing like a tree" and then the "beach ball" pose, gradually increasing the times. After about six weeks I began to notice some changes. I cannot say what the exact time frame was of each event, because I was not anticipating them.

Suddenly, one day while doing the "beach ball" pose, I realized that I had more energy. Prior to that, after playing tennis in the morning, I would be pretty much wiped out for the rest of the day. Now I had energy for other things, which included things like more yoga exercises and gardening.

Next, I noticed my sense of smell improved. I realized that we had a scented candle in one bathroom. While watching TV, I noticed that it didn't matter if I wore glasses or not. Also, my night vision while driving had vastly improved with the glasses off. The next time I went to the DMV for a driver's license renewal, I passed the eye test without glasses for the first time in 45 years. Since I could read all the letters on the eye chart, the tester assumed that I had memorized all the eye charts. Lately, I have noticed that my eyes seem brighter, livelier, and bluer after standing meditation sessions. My wife also noticed the bluer eyes. There are a lot of people in their 40's and 50's who have eye problems and could no doubt benefit from standing meditation.

My wife casually mentioned that I must be having my hair dyed, when I got a haircut. The lady who has cut my hair for the last 20 years also confirmed that my hair had gone back to its more natural color. From my high school class reunion pictures I noticed that all my former classmates had gray or white hair. Typically, my age is guessed to be 10-15 years younger than it is.

I believe that, according to western medicine, there are some very good reasons for these things happening. Standing meditation promotes the flow of cerebrospinal fluid in the spine and brain. Two very excellent articles that can be found on the Internet are by Dr. Don Glassey, a chiropractor, relating to cerebrospinal fluid flow, "Why Yoga Works," and "Life Energy and Healing." According to Dr. Glassey there is a cerebrospinal fluid pump right behind the nose. This might explain why the sense of smell, eyesight, and hair color would be favorably affected. In books on tai chi, it is mentioned that it is not unusual for a person's hair color to return to its more natural color by doing standing meditation. When doing standing meditation, a great deal of heat is generated by the body, which tells me something is definitely going on.

While doing the standing meditation, I could feel energy in my hands and arms. After a while, I could feel the energy flowing along my spine. Playing tennis one day, there was a particularly long point. A player sitting on the bench asked why I wasn't winded. It was clear that I had more stamina. One day we had to wait for a tennis court and to kill time, I stood under a pine tree and did the "beach ball" pose for about 10-15 minutes. The first set I made no errors, amazing. Lately, I have not been that thrilled with my tennis game. Most of the players that I play tennis with are on the courts four or more times a week whereas I only play twice a week. Recently, I have started coming to the courts ten minutes early and stand under a large pine tree with my back to the sun doing the hold the beach ball pose. My serve, movement, and ground strokes are noticeably better, strange, but true.

A Chinese tennis player asked me one day why I didn't have any ailments or injuries. Nearly all the players were retired, and they all seemed to have some sort of health problem. I told him about standing meditation. Both he and his wife took it up. His wife felt energy right away at the top of her head, which is a very positive sign. He also reported that their sex life was better.

Anyone who plays tennis knows, that win or lose, you usually feel good coming off the court. One reason for this, I believe, is that you are usually in a state of alert awareness while playing, especially in doubles. If you aren't, you are liable to catch a tennis ball in the midsection. Also, the net man is normally in a stationary pose, which is similar to a standing meditation pose.

The Way of Energy book says that fir trees give off a lot of energy or chi. My wife and I go to a Starbucks and sit in the car under large pine and redwood trees and have our coffee. We both notice the feeling of energy, different from the caffeine effect.

After 12 years of going to an ophthalmologist every two years because of an eye problem when I was 60, the doctor said he no longer needed to see me. He seemed disappointed. I had tried to convince him, to no avail, that standing meditation was good for the eyes.

For a few years I was going to the dentist's office three times a year to get my teeth cleaned. The dental hygienist said, that I only needed to come twice a year as my gums looked great, and whatever I was doing for them, keep doing it.

Another aspect of standing meditation is that I lost my desire to drink alcoholic beverages. Coffee no longer has the hold on me that it used to. I only have maybe one or two cups a week.

I was fortunate to have a tai chi instructor who was also a kung fu master. As part of the class, we would do standing meditation. He was very sold on standing meditation for kung fu fighters and had many stories to tell about him and his kung fu grandmaster, Y. C. Wong, going to the Shaolin Temple in China for additional training every year where standing meditation is also taught. No matter what I told him, he could come up with more impressive stories about what people can do using standing meditation. He told about someone at the temple that would be in the hold the beach ball pose 16 hours a day. When he would be conversing with someone, he would be in the pose. Another individual would sell energy. To deliver the energy, he would stand a few feet in front of you and would move two fingers down the length of your torso. My tai chi instructor said that advanced students could feel the energy in their bones while doing meditation. These stories would be shared before or after class. Unfortunately, he didn't emphasize standing meditation in class.

For the last twelve years, I have been virtually free of any illnesses. One of the reasons, I believe, is that in the "holding the beach ball pose" a circle of energy is generated in front of the thymus gland and that helps the thymus strengthen the immune system. About every other year, I would get the stomach flu, which would usually take about three days to fully recover from. The last time I got stomach flu; I recovered in about an hour. I had a stretch of several years of not having stomach flu.

Also, I have tremendously more energy, which allows me to do the standing meditation twice a day for at least 30 minutes, yoga sessions twice a day, two or three visits to the health club a week, which includes yoga classes, weight workouts, treadmill work, two tennis games a week, gardening, etc. I now get an hour and a half less of sleep a night and could probably get by with less.

If I have trouble remembering something like someone's name, I try to recall it while doing standing meditation. The answer usually comes to mind.

It is strange that some tai chi instructors are unaware of the benefits of standing meditation. Maybe the fact that it only takes five minutes to teach it to someone has something to do with it, not good for full employment. For several years, I took tai chi classes twice a week but really didn't think I was gaining much from the classes. One instructor was actually hostile to the idea of standing meditation, and asked me not to discuss it with other students during class breaks!

It is interesting to note that while watching a fund raising program on a PBS TV station there were two yoga instructors on. One of the instructors said quietly that all you need to do is the "mountain pose," which looks very similar to a standing meditation pose. If that were true, it would put an awful lot of yoga instructors out of business.

CHAPTER 19

FINANCIAL SUCCESS

EVERYONE WOULD LIKE to obtain some measure of financial security in life. There are some simple guidelines that go a long way toward obtaining that goal. Number one is to invest your savings in real estate. Buy a home as soon as you possibly can financially swing it. Stay away from the stock market unless you have some very special or unique talents. Do not lend money to relatives; they will not repay you and in the end there will be only animosity. A loan to a relative should be treated as a gift in most cases. Try to find a job that has some kind of retirement program. When you do retire, you will have a home mostly paid for or completely paid off and have a substantial equity. Not having a house payment is a very big plus toward financial security after retirement. Your social security check and your retirement pay should cover most of your expenses. Despite breaking most of these rules, I was able to persevere by working in high paying jobs, mostly overseas. One of the smartest things that I did on retirement was to take out a company-sponsored annuity instead of trying to make a larger amount through bonds or other investments. Having a steady, guaranteed income makes one sleep better at night.

CHAPTER **20**

YOGA

LIKE MANY THINGS that a person becomes knowledgeable of, you find out that people, who are supposed to know, don't always impart the most helpful information. Yoga is a good example of this. After many years of not making much progress on backward bending doing yoga poses and taking yoga classes, I started using an inflatable ball and footstool for backward bending. In a very short time, my backward bending ability improved dramatically. My back muscles also became much stronger and the headstand is easier to get into and come down out of now. Backward bending is very energizing. The very best yoga exercise is believed by many to be the headstand. It is called the "King of Asanas (poses)" in B.K.S. Iyengar's classic book "Light on Yoga." I do the headstand exercise twice a day. Yet, most health clubs and yoga studios do not teach the headstand. I believe that there must be concern of possible lawsuits, if there are back problems.

One of the main goals of yoga is to quiet the mind to increase awareness and facilitate the flow of energy, yet the quieting of the mind is not usually mentioned in yoga classes. The ultimate goal of yoga is to raise the kundalini energy up the spine. If you were to ask most yoga students what kundalini is, they wouldn't know. It is unfathomable that yoga instructors never mention the subject. Very useful things like the "breath of fire" are not explained and not often taught. There are many yoga studios and health clubs in any large community in southern California, but it is hard to find convenient classes in kundalini yoga. Buying a good kundalini DVD helps. The focus of kundalini yoga is on exercising the spine, which promotes the flow of energy through the spine. Even a casual student of yoga should find a way to take classes in kundalini yoga. Spinal exercises are for the most part very easy to do. Recently, I started doing six simple spinal exercises of fifteen repetitions each while in a sitting position. Four months later I had my annual physical examination. In reviewing my lab test results with the doctor it turns out my creatin (kidney function test) was down to 1.5 from 1.7 and my PSA number for the prostrate was unbelievably low at 1.3; for me it typically ran around 4.0. Since then I have added three more exercises that benefit the spine and trunk. The whole scenario takes around six minutes. I don't know of anyone who can't find six minutes in there daily routine. At my last annual physical my creatin level improved by another 0.1 and my PSA number was even lower at 0.9. The exercises also make you feel more alive. Lately, I have noticed that my reflexes are better, i.e., my reaction time in tennis to balls hit right at me at the net in doubles has improved. It has always been good, but even the opponents have been commenting on my improved quickness.

Unfortunately, most yoga classes are just exercise classes. It is admirable to be able to twist your body in all kinds of very difficult poses and hold the pose for seemingly endless amounts of time. One of the favorites of yoga instructors is the "down dog" pose, which we seem to do endlessly in some classes. I have yet to find a good reason for spending so much time in "down dog." After doing yoga for 45 years, I question the emphasis. In my opinion, exercising the spine along with the headstand and shoulder stand are the most valuable yoga exercises that you can do, and that is where the focus should lie. In some classes we do a little of this and a little of that; the end result is no improvement in flexibility and probably not a great deal of benefit other than to get some exercise.

A group of 16 men played doubles tennis one evening a week, and after playing round robin with a different partner each week, the four players with the best won/loss records would play in a championship match. I thought that I did well to finish in the middle of the pack. The next season I would spend about 20 minutes doing yoga exercises before I played. That season I finished number two. The number one player was obviously the best player. He and I rather easily beat the second placed team in the playoff.

CHAPTER 21

OBSERVATIONS

MOVING ON TO a more philosophical subject. It has always been a mystery why some people are totally aware of what is going on around them and others have absolutely no clue. Unawareness extends to driving a car of which we are all too familiar with. We should try not to be to frustrated with other drivers. At the super market, you see elderly shoppers who can barely maneuver their shopping carts, and then they get in their cars and drive home, scary. It seems that some people are unaware that there are two sexes, which gets worse the older they are. Intelligence is definitely involved, but it is more than that. There are also different levels of awareness. According to Swami Durgananda in "Heart of Meditation," you need to spend one and one half to three hours a day in meditation to develop awareness. In fact, she says ultimately that there is only awareness! It is interesting to note that the founder of the Christian Science Church, Mary Baker Eddy, who preformed hundreds of documented healings, meditated three hours a day.

Recently, after doing a morning yoga session of about two hours, I started my standing meditation. It soon became apparent that I was in some kind of altered state in that there was only awareness of my surroundings with no thoughts of any kind. Now I realized that many years ago while a college student, after lengthy studying sessions, I had obtained a similar state. On a few occasions the instructor and other students would comment on, for lack of a better description, the totally relaxed state that I was in. Enlightenment has been described as a state of pure awareness.

If you spend any time at health clubs, you will probably notice that most of the the male customers focus almost entirely on improving strength and muscle mass along with some cardio work. That is great if you plan to enter a bodybuilding contest or become a gigolo. Of equal and really greater importance, especially as you get older, is to improve your balance and flexibility. Even something as simple as a few minutes a day of free form dancing, where you twist and bend, would go a long ways towards improving spinal flexibility. Standing on one foot is very good for improving balance. There are many exercises that improve balance. One of my favorites is to bounce on a trampoline on one foot, which also improves leg strength. There are countless tales of people being seriously hurt or even dying from falling. Exercising and flexing the spine, as was discussed earlier, promotes the flow of cerebrospinal fluid, which any chiropractor will tell you is the key to good health. I was at the Ventura County Courthouse for jury duty not long ago. I went to step over a low retaining wall onto a patio while reading a book. Little did I realize that the ground level on the other side of the wall was two feet lower! After some acrobatics on one foot, I managed to stay upright with no strain or damage other than to my dignity.

If you talk to tennis players, they will probably tell you that they are flexible. Compared to the types of things that you try to do in advanced yoga classes, the flexibility gained playing tennis is a joke. Maybe no one needs to be that flexible, but the yoga students that I know look awfully healthy. Most yoga classes have a good cardio component.

CHAPTER 22

INMATES RUNNING THE ASYLUM

MY WIFE AND I were tennis members at a very nice country club for 15 years. The members bought the club and soon things began to change. The major problem for us was that my wife, who had played successfully in the tennis leagues, was suddenly not allowed to play. She was not even allowed to pay to play in group practice clinics. I wrote a letter to the club president stating that the value of our membership had substantially decreased and suggested that my wife be reinstated to play in the tennis leagues, the club refund our purchase price, or we will go to Small Claims Court. The actual resale value of the membership had decreased by about two thirds. I received a nasty and threatening written response. Considering that the club president was a partner in a law firm, such a response was astounding. I tried to get the past club president, who had been our stock broker for many years and who had talked us into buying a club membership, to intercede; but he begged off.

Out of spite, I gave the story to the newspapers, who had a field day with it. Anything that I said was printed in the newspapers as gospel truth. It was even on the radio news. The country club got a few million dollars worth of bad publicity. The bottom line was that the country club lost in small claims court, after which they appealed to superior court. On our court date five club officers plus a hired attorney marched into the courtroom in their dark, pin stripped suits.

Bring it on! Their attorney sauntered over, and we settled out of court for about 90% of what I was asking. Considering the cost of the attorney, it would have been cheaper if they had not appealed. There is a saying that a bad settlement in better than rolling the dice in a courtroom. The moral to the story is to be very leery of any situation where the inmates are running the asylum. Our former country club now charges an arm and a leg in monthly dues to be a member. One must sell the membership to escape. It has been determined in court that you cannot simply walk away. For the golf members the monthly dues are astronomical.

For many years, I have coordinated men's doubles games on public tennis courts in a park. If a player is difficult, which happens, or unreliable, he is not asked to play again. The courts we play on are very nice and, generally speaking, the people who play on public courts are nicer and friendlier than tennis club members, strange but true. There are no golf balls whizzing by during play as has happened at two country clubs that my wife and I have belonged to. There are a large number of people playing tennis in there 70's and 80's and many of them move extremely well around the court. I played tennis regularly with a player who was 90 and he played about the same as he did thirty years ago.

CHAPTER **23**

UFO,s ETC.

ONE OF THE luxuries of retirement is that you have time to delve into things that you never had time for before. One such topic that I started reading up on was UFOs. After reading numerous books on the subject and researching on the Internet, it became apparent that intelligently controlled aircraft are present in our skies. Even a casual investigation would convince most thinking individuals that they exist. Our government officials are deniers, unlike European and South American countries, because they no doubt think that the public will want something done about the situation, and government is really powerless to do anything. Actually, the government looks even worse by pretending that they don't exist. The news media also will not take the subject seriously, but then journalism majors never were the brightest candles on the cake.

Another topic of interest is the subject of near death experiences. With the improvement in resuscitating patients, who have suffered some kind of trauma, the number of near death experiences has skyrocketed. One author claims to have investigated 10,000 cases. It is interesting that a very large percentage of those persons who have had the experience have no fear of death. My own wife had such an experience during childbirth, and yes, she has no fear of death. On a related subject, reincarnation is accepted as fact by a large portion of the world's population. Yet the Christian religions will not touch the subject. Again there is overwhelming evidence that people have lived before. Going to a reputable hypno-therapist, who does past life regression, can give you a totally new prospective on your present life. Dr. Brian L. Weiss, a psychiatrist, has written extensively on past life regression and future life viewing using hypnosis, which he uses for treatment of his patients.

Perhaps the greatest fear people have is the fear of death. There is a psychic that believes that our higher selves decide when we should leave this earth. If the general public accepted that idea, it would greatly relieve a lot of unnecessary stress in the world.

Speaking of unnecessary stress, there is a certain segment of humanity whose purpose in life seems to be to annoy and irritate other people. These toxic people spend their time making negative, critical, or combative remarks and doing hurtful things. Avoid these destructive people whether they are relatives, friends, fellow workers or whoever. One good way of determining if someone is your friend is to tell a positive story about something that you have done and gauge the reaction. Also, tell something negative and listen to their comments.

A point, which is lost on much of the population, is to never stop learning. It always mystified me why people would stop growing intellectually. It happens as early as when they graduate from high school. I always thought it was fun to learn or do something new. When you try to share some bit of information with people, you can often see the glazed look come into their eyes. There seems to be a reluctance to learn or try anything new. If someone has known you for a long time, many seem to think that you can't possibly know something of value that they don't know. This was very prevalent in the work environment, where higher-level managers often took the attitude that if what you were saying had any value, they would already know it. I found that good ideas sometimes came from the most unlikely sources. There are, of course, notable exceptions. You probably have a lot of respect for someone who actually listens. Oddly enough, total strangers often listen intently to what you have to say. I guess they figure that if you take the time to mention something, it just might have some value.

One final suggestion is to read something positive every day. I no longer can watch the morning news on television; every story is such a downer. It helps to say to myself what can I do better today.

CPSIA information can be obtained
at www.ICGtesting.com
Printed in the USA
FSOW01n1655250217
31230FS

9 781478 746515